healthy eating during
menopause

Dr. Marilyn Glenville PhD with
Lewis Esson

healthy eating during
menopause

Photography by Ian Wallace

Kyle Books

This edition published by Kyle Books in 2009, an imprint of Kyle Cathie Limited
www.kylecathie.com
Distributed by National Book Network
4501 Forbes Blvd., Suite 200, Lanham, MD 20706
Phone: (301) 459 3366

First published in the U.S. in 2004 by Barnes & Noble Books

ISBN 978-1-906868-03-1

First published in Great Britain in 2004 by Kyle Cathie Ltd

Originally published in 2000 as *Natural Alternatives to HRT Cookbook*. Subsequently published in 2002 as *Eat Your Way Through the Menopause*.

10 9 8 7 6 5 4 3 2 1

Marilyn Glenville is hereby identified as the author of this work in accordance with Section 77 of the Copyright, Designs and Patents Act 1988.

Text © 2000 and 2004 Marilyn Glenville
Photography © 2000 Ian Wallace, with the exception of those photographs listed on the right.

Book design © 2004 Kyle Cathie Limited

Recipes by Lewis Esson
Senior Editor Muna Reyal
Designer Carl Hodson
Photographer Ian Wallace, *see also* right
Home economist Louise Pickford
Styling Helen Trent
Edited by Candida Hall
Editorial Assistant Jennifer Wheatley
Production Sha Huxtable and Alice Holloway

Library of Congress Control Number: 2009924511

Color reproduction by Sang Choy
Printed and bound in Singapore by Star Standard

contents

dedication

To Mum, Dad, and sister Janet for all those happy memories

important note

- With 123 delicious recipes, covering every meal of the day including Breakfasts and Brunches, Soups, Appetizers, and Snacks, Lunches and Light Meals, Main Courses, Side Dishes, Desserts, Breads, Cakes, and Cookies, and Basic Recipes, this book is a comprehensive guide to healthy eating during menopause.

- Dr. Marilyn Glenville, an authority on women's health and menopause, gives advice on what to eat, highlighting the importance of a diet rich in essential fatty acids, polyunsaturated fats, and phytoestrogens. She also explains what to avoid during menopause, and why. Packed with shopping and cooking tips, this is the only guide you will ever need during menopause.

- In *Healthy Eating during Menopause*, Dr. Marilyn Glenville shows you how your diet can work as a natural alternative to HRT and give you results far superior to any drug. HRT is a controversial and much-debated issue and this book shows how menopause can be treated naturally through diet, without risks, or side effects.

- Part of a Healthy Eating series which includes *Healthy Gluten-free Eating*, *Healthy Dairy-free Eating*, *Healthy Eating for your Heart*, *Healthy Eating for Lower Cholesterol,* and *Healthy Eating for Diabetes*.

introduction

What is menopause?

Menopause is a natural event, not an illness. It is a transition from one stage of our lives into another.

Medically speaking, menopause is your very last period. When we talk about menopause we normally mean the transition period, or the "change of life,"which can span 15 to 20 years and the medical terminology for this time is the "climacteric."

When does menopause happen?

The average age in the US is 51, which means that as many women go through menopause before this age as afterwards. If it happens before the age of 40, it is classed as premature menopause.

The timing of menopause can be linked to a number of factors. The age at which your mother reached menopause can be a good guide. But some factors such as smoking can bring on earlier menopause, so if your mother smoked and you don't, or vice versa, the timing of your menopause may be completely different from hers.

Why does the menopause happen?

During menopause you literally run out of eggs. You are born with your store of eggs numbering about 2 million. As you go

through puberty, you have about 750,000 eggs and by the age of 45, about 10,000 may be left. Menopause occurs when your store of eggs is completely depleted.

What symptoms could you experience?

Many symptoms are associated with menopause. These can include:

* hot flashes
* night sweats
* irritability
* declining libido
* osteoporosis
* weight gain
* vaginal dryness
* aging skin
* changes in hair quality
* headaches
* mood swings
* depression
* lack of energy
* joint pains
* hair loss

For many women the only symptoms they experience are hot flashes and night sweats. Others can experience a number of completely different ones. Some of the above symptoms are also just a natural part of the aging process and can affect middle-aged men just as much as they affect women – think of irritability, declining libido, weight gain, aging skin, depression, and anxiety. It is therefore important not to blame everything on menopause.

There are also some women who sail through menopause. They do not experience any symptoms and all that happens is their periods stop.

What treatments are available?

Menopause is often seen as a deficiency disease in that we reach a certain age and our hormones decline. So by replacing hormones with Hormone Replacement Therapy (HRT) we have a treatment for menopause. HRT was introduced in the 1930s and medically has become a popular treatment for menopausal symptoms. However, in the last few years a number of good clinical trials have shown that the risks of taking HRT, in terms of higher risks of breast cancer, heart disease, strokes, and thrombosis, do not outweigh the benefits.

We also know from research into other cultures that menopause is not experienced in the same way by all women. Research has also shown that in those cultures the women have a lower risk of breast cancer, heart disease and osteoporosis, which are long-term health risks for women.

The key to healthy menopause is to eat foods that will help to control the symptoms of hot flushes, night sweats, vaginal dryness, mood swings, lack of libido, joint pains, aging skin, and lackluster hair. Quite simply, the correct diet can not only help to reduce these symptoms and prevent osteoporosis but also protect you against heart disease and breast cancer.

food and menopause

Yes, you can literally eat your way through menopause. In research into other cultures, scientists have found that menopause is not experienced in the same way by all women. Therefore the question arises as to what most differentiates these women from us in the Western world. The answer is our diet. In some cultures, like Japan, women also have one sixth the rate of breast cancer that we have. Studies in the USA have shown that when Japanese women move to the West and adopt a Western diet, they develop a breast cancer rate similar to ours. So it is not a genetic factor particular to Japanese women but something in their diet that distinguishes them.

People's attitudes to menopause also vary enormously around the world. In some cultures it is seen as a positive change: freedom from the need for contraception, freedom from the monthly bleed, and the arrival of a new status of "wise woman." Yet in our society it is usually seen as a time of loss.

Logic dictates that if we add back these hormones we have a "cure" – surely? After all, diabetes is the result of a hormone deficiency – when the hormone insulin is not sufficient to maintain normal blood sugar levels – and all that is needed is for insulin to be supplied from outside and the imbalance is corrected. Thus it is suggested that menopause and diabetes are similar. But diabetes is an illness, menopause is not. All women are going to go through menopause, but we are not all going to get diabetes.

Unfortunately, although menopause is a natural event, there is a lot of pressure on women to take HRT. This is usually done with an aspect of fear, with the implication that if we don't take HRT our bones will crumble, our skin will sag, our hair will become dry, we'll age more quickly, lose our sex drive, and suffer from vaginal dryness. It is hard for any woman to resist that kind of pressure.

But over the years research has shown that there is a negative side to HRT, with numerous studies showing an increased risk of breast cancer. The final nail in the coffin was in the summer of 2002, when a major research program from the Women's Health Initiative was abandoned. The research program on 27,000 women, was due to run for eight years but was canceled after five years as it showed that women taking HRT had a 26 percent higher risk of breast cancer, a 41 percent increase in the chance of a stroke and a 29 percent increased heart risk.[1]

For many women, this risk is not acceptable. Also, some women have come to me complaining of side effects of HRT such as weight gain (sometimes up to 28 pounds) and an uncomfortable increase in bra size by up to two cups.

Women want and have demanded another way of dealing with menopause, one which does not carry these unacceptable risks and side effects and yet prevents osteoporosis and alleviates menopausal symptoms. Quite simply, the correct diet cannot only help to reduce these

symptoms and prevent osteoporosis but also protect you against heart disease and breast cancer.

Numerous medical articles are currently being published showing the health benefits of substances called phytoestrogens. These phytoestrogens, or plant hormones, are contained naturally in certain everyday foods which have a huge influence on how women experience menopause. In our "fast food" society we have moved away from these traditional foods and are now paying the price in terms of our health. By using the simple, inspiring recipes in this book you will help alleviate the symptoms of menopause by increasing your intake of highly beneficial – and delicious – ingredients.

Heart disease is the West's biggest killer, particularly of men. Eating the foods described in this book can also reduce the risk of heart disease. Prostate cancer is another serious killer, with four times more men dying from it than women from cancer of the cervix. Yet Japanese men have a lower death rate for prostate cancer than men in the UK. Why? Evidence points to the fact that the Japanese eat good quantities of foods like soy (one of the phytoestrogens) every day.

These phytoestrogens have a balancing effect on hormones in both men and women, so, not only do menopausal women benefit from the advice and recipes in this book, but the men in their lives do too. The book is invaluable for any family that wants to enjoy eating their way to optimum health.

understanding the role of estrogen

Estrogen is the key hormone responsible for the transition from childhood to womanhood. It causes the breasts to develop and produces our characteristic feminine shape. It also causes the lining of the womb (uterus) to thicken each month in anticipation of receiving a fertilized egg. The average age of menopause in the US is 51 but symptoms associated with menopause such as hot flashes, night sweats, etc., can all start well before your periods stop. As you get nearer to menopause, ovulation (when an egg is released) becomes less likely each month because estrogen levels are beginning to decline. However, as they will still have a period most women won't know they have not ovulated.

During actual menopause, when you have your last period, you have literally run out of eggs. But contrary to popular opinion, the menopausal ovary is not a dead or dying organ. It continues to produce estrogen, although in smaller quantities, for at least 12 years after the start of menopause. (The start is considered to be the moment when hormone production begins to decline.) In addition, the adrenal glands (which sit on top of the kidneys) produce estrogen, which is used alongside the ovaries' diminishing supply. Body fat is also a manufacturing plant for estrogen. Fat produces estrogen all our lives – which is why low- or no-fat diets, so often recommended for slimmers, can be a big mistake for women.

As women, we need estrogen to protect our bones and heart. Nature is always trying to maintain a balance because there are problems if estrogen levels are either too low or too high. If we don't have enough our bones and heart are not protected, and if we have too much we risk breast cancer.

Because body fat is a manufacturing plant for estrogen, if you are overweight your estrogen levels will be higher than normal. It is fine to become slightly heavier during menopause since this extra estrogen from the fat cells balances the estrogen decline from the ovaries. However, being very overweight brings with it excess estrogen levels, which can mean increased risks of breast and womb cancer. Both breast and womb cancer are estrogen-sensitive, meaning that estrogen can stimulate cancer cells and can actually grow in the presence of this hormone. Eestrogen's role in the body is as a "builder," helping to build the lining of the womb in the first half of the menstrual cycle. If this "building" mechanism goes out of control, then increased cell growth could lead to an estrogen-dependent tumor and sometimes cancer.

Other conditions that are affected by high estrogen levels include endometriosis (when the lining of the womb grows in places other than just the womb), fibroids (benign tumors in the womb), heavy and/or long periods, and fibrocystic breast disease (lumpy and tender breasts). Eating healthy foods, such as the recipes in this book, will help to control your weight naturally without having to diet, which doesn't work anyway. If you need extra help with weight loss, my book *Natural Alternatives to Dieting* will be useful.

"Good" and "bad" estrogens

There are "good" and "bad" estrogens, in terms of whether they are carcinogenic or not. Estrogen is not one -hormone but several grouped together, including estradiol, estrone, and estriol. All three estrogens have the same beneficial effects on our skin and vagina and protect the heart and bones. The oestrogens vary in strength – with oestradiol being the most carcinogenic. It is the liver's job to convert estradiol and estrone into estriol (the least carcinogenic estrogen) so it is especially important that your liver is working efficiently as you get older.

Each estrogen is active at different stages of our reproductive lives. Estradiol is very active during our adolescent years, but as menopause approaches production of it declines. Around this time the adrenal glands and estrogen-producing fat cells are producing estrone instead.

The estrogen in HRT

If you decide to take HRT, you are adding back estrogen in its most carcinogenic form (estradiol) precisely at the time when your body is naturally reducing its supply of estradiol. You are therefore asking a lot of your liver to convert this more powerful estrogen into weaker estriol and to excrete it from your body.

Estrogen therapy has existed since the 1930s when it was given in the form of an injection. By 1938, estrogen implants were introduced, which were more convenient. However, it soon became clear that supplying estrogen alone could increase the risk of cancer of the womb and breasts. When research studies demonstrated that this increased risk could be up to seven times higher than normal for womb cancer, there was panic. As mentioned above, estrogen builds up the lining of the womb ready to receive a fertilized egg, so logically, if estrogen is added on its own without the womb lining being shed each month, there is a real chance of overproduction of the cells lining the womb and of possible mutation. So in the early 1980s scientists added progestogen (the synthetic version of progesterone) to the hormone therapy in order to protect the womb lining from overstimulation and subsequent cancer. And so ERT (Estrogen Replacement Therapy) became HRT, as it no longer contained estrogen only.

There still remains the risk of womb cancer even with combined HRT (estrogen and progestogen) but it is smaller than with pure estrogen therapy. The risks of developing breast cancer from taking HRT are now well known and have been confirmed in a number of studies.[1]

Due to the links made between HRT and cancer, research is under way into the possibility of creating a much more targeted drug that would stimulate certain estrogen receptors but avoid any detrimental effect on the breasts and womb. The drug would function as an estrogen promoter in organs where estrogen is needed and beneficial (e.g., the heart and bones) while acting as an "anti-estrogen" in organs where unnecessary estrogen can be dangerous (e.g., the breast and womb). This new generation of HRT is called SERMS (Selective Eestrogen Receptor Modulators). The relatively new drug raloxifene is one of these, but its full potential is still being examined. Possible side effects include increased clots and even an increase in hot flashes! So it is unfortunately useless in the treatment of hot flashes or hot sweats; instead it is aimed at those women who want protection for their bones without running the risk of breast cancer. As yet, therefore, we must continue waiting for the ultimate designer drug for menopause.

Living in a "sea of hormones"

We are also exposed to estrogens from the environment. There are estrogen-like chemicals that come from pesticides or plastics called xenoestrogens (foreign estrogens) which have been linked to changes in wildlife. Just how potent these xenoestrogens are was discovered by a group of scientists who found that alligators which had hatched in Lake Apopka, Florida, had abnormally small penises and altered hormonal levels. They linked these findings with the fact that in 1980 there had been a massive spill of kelthane, a pesticide, into the lake. The xenoestrogens from the pesticide were feminizing the alligators.

Xenoestrogens enter the body through food and drink but can also enter our skin from toiletries such as skin creams and lotions. These xenoestrogens are then stored in body fat, with overweight people tending to have a higher concentration because xenoestrogens are lipophilic – fat-loving. Xenoestrogens can affect men and women differently. Women with higher concentrations of certain organo-chlorine pesticides in their bodies run a greater risk of developing breast cancer than women with lower levels. Girls in the West are now entering puberty earlier than they did in past generations, which may be partly due to the influence of xenoestrogens. At the turn of the century the average age was 15; nowadays some girls as young as eight are growing breasts and pubic hair.

As for men, there are concerns that xenoestrogens are responsible for the decrease in sperm counts by 50 percent in the West over the last ten years. There has also been a rise in testicular and prostate cancer, and even breast cancer. More young boys are now born with undescended testes and other reproductive problems.

How can you reduce levels of xenoestrogens?

The food industry has become reliant on pesticides. There are several thousand brands of insecticide, herbicide, and fungicide which are approved for use in the US, and some fruit and vegetables are sprayed as many as ten times before they reach the supermarket shelves.

To reduce your own intake of xenoestrogens, where possible, you should try to buy organic produce. With concern over BSE (Bovine spongiform encephalopathy) and genetically modified food (see page 36) there is increasing public demand for organic foods, which is also helping to bring prices down. Organic foods are generally free of genetically modified ingredients, antibiotics, and growth hormones and should contain higher amounts of vitamins and minerals – particularly vital micronutrients like zinc as they are grown on more nutrient-rich soil.

You may know a friend who owns an garden or a local farmer who grows vegetables.There may be local companies that could deliver a box of organic produce to your home every week. Otherwise most supermarkets have an excellent range of organic produce. Some have tasty vegetables and organic breads to choose from. Others now have a section of organic packaged foods including organic tomato ketchup, spaghetti sauce, mayonnaise etc. If you are on a tight budget, try at least to buy organic grains such as brown rice, oats etc., or organic whole-wheat bread. This is because the smaller the food, such as rice or wheat, the more pesticides it can absorb as compared with a carrot or potato for example.

If your vegetables and fruit are not organic, wash them thoroughly. You can buy washes from health food stores which claim to be able to remove farm chemicals, waxes, and surface grime. Washing cannot alter the amount of pesticides inherently absorbed into the vegetables, but it can at least take away surface residues.

It is not only pesticides but also plastics that can mimic estrogen, so you should also try to reduce your exposure to plastics. One scientist in the Boston was studying breast cancer cells and stored them in plastic test tubes. Then one day these cancer cells started to divide and multiply of their own accord, just as if estrogen were present. On analysis of the tubes it was found that they contained nonylphenol, which is one of the family of alkylphenols that are used in paints, toiletries, agricultural chemicals, and detergents. As soon as they changed the tubes, the effect stopped.

Try to avoid as much as possible food and drinks in plastic containers or wrapped in plastic, especially fatty foods, because the xenoestrogens are lipophilic. Remove food from plastic packaging as soon as possible. Do not heat food in plastic, particularly in a microwave oven. Store your food in the fridge in a glass dish covered with a glass lid or saucer rather than plastic wrap.

Where can you get beneficial estrogens from?

Naturally, all of us want the beneficial effects of estrogen – soft skin, strong bones, a healthy heart, etc., – without running the risk of developing cancer from taking steroid hormones (which is, after all, what HRT is). Even better, we would like to receive the cancer-protection effects of estrogen. Marvelously, it is possible to do this, just by eating! Sounds too simple to be true? Well, it really is simple. The "good" estrogens that we require are phytoestrogens, or plant hormones, and they naturally occur in certain foods. By maintaining a healthy diet of phytoestrogen-rich foods, we can mirror what women in traditional cultures such as India and Japan have been doing for centuries and, like them, enjoy strong bones, healthy hearts, and minimal menopausal symptoms. The next section explains how this is possible.

what you need to eat during menopause

This section covers the foods that you need to eat before and during menopause in order to achieve specific health benefits. These foods are so easy to incorporate into your daily meals that you will wonder why we are not all eating like this anyway – and that means the whole family. For each group of foods an explanation is given as to their importance during menopause and the effect they will have on your body.

Many foods are recommended for one particular benefit, yet also contain other valuable qualities. Soy is a good example of this. Not only does it have valuable levels of phytoestrogens but it also contains good levels of essential fatty acids, has antioxidant properties, is virtually saturated fat-free, and has excellent levels of vegetable protein and a good fiber content. There are many other foods like this, but in general I have focussed on their principal beneficial qualities.

Follow this book's advice in order to:

∗ control menopausal symptoms like hot flashes, night sweats, vaginal dryness, lack of sex drive, lack of energy, mood swings
∗ prevent osteoporosis
∗ maintain a healthy heart
∗ protect against cancer
∗ minimize aching joints and stiffness
∗ prevent degenerative diseases like arthritis
∗ bring you good mental health
∗ slow down the aging process
∗ control weight naturally – no need for dieting
∗ aim for optimum health, which in turn will give you a good quality of life so that you have enough energy for your needs, healthy sleep, and a zest for living

Can all of this be achieved just by eating certain foods? The answer is yes, and it is all backed up by scientific studies.

Phytoestrogens – plant hormones

Phytoestrogens ("phyto" meaning plant) are naturally occurring substances in food that have a hormone-like action. Almost all fruit, vegetables, and cereals contain phyto-strogens in varying strengths and composition, but it is the isoflavones (one of the classes of phytoestrogens) that are the most beneficial kind. These are found in legumes such as soy, lentils, chickpeas, etc. In the human gut, bacteria convert isoflavones into substances that have an estrogenic action, although they are not themselves hormones.

An average Japanese woman's daily intake of isoflavones is between 20 and 80mg per day, Asian women's diets about 45mg per day, while American and British women

---

Foods that contain phytoestrogens

The following foods are sources of phytoestrogens, but tests are still under way to determine their isoflavone content. At the moment it is known that legumes contain good levels of isoflavones, and soy ranks the highest.

∗ Soy
∗ Other legumes such as lentils, chickpeas, adzuki beans, kidney beans, peas
∗ Garlic
∗ Celery

∗ Seeds, including linseeds, sesame, pumpkin, poppy, caraway, sunflower
∗ Grains like rice, oats, wheat, barley, rye
∗ Fruit, including apples, plums, cherries, cranberries, citrus fruits
∗ Vegetables, including broccoli, carrots, rhubarb, potatoes
∗ Sprouts like alfafa and mung bean sprouts
∗ Some herbs and spices are also classed as phytoestrogens, including cinnamon, sage, red clover, hops, fennel, parsley

generally consume between 1–3mg per day, with a recent study showing that healthy post-menopausal Caucasian women in the US were consuming less than 1mg per day – quite a difference.[1]

Tests show that Japanese women have as much as 100–1,000 times higher levels of isoflavones in their urine and plasma than the amount found among British and American women. This indicates that their traditional soy-high diet supplies them naturally with the phytonutrients (plant compounds) that may prevent hormonally linked cancers.[2]

Phytoestrogens can be broken down into a number of classes, including:

Isoflavones

These are found in high concentration in legumes such as lentils, chickpeas, and soybeans, which are particularly rich in isoflavones. There are four important types of isoflavones contained in food: genistein, daidzein, biochanin A, and formononetin. Chickpeas and lentils contain all four types, while soy contains just genistein and daidzein.

Lignans

These are found in almost all cereals and vegetables, but with the highest concentrations in the oilseeds, especially linseeds (flax).

Coumestans

These types of phytoestrogens are found mainly in alfafa and mung bean sprouts.

Soy

Soybeans are especially rich in phytoe-strogens and so have been studied extensively. Soy contains two isoflavone compounds called genistein and daidzein, which make up approximately 75 percent of the soybean protein.

Soybeans contain more protein than cows' milk without the saturated fat or cholesterol. They are also the only food considered to be a complete protein because they contain all eight essential amino acids. Soy is also high in essential fatty acids and soy milk is naturally cholesterol-free.

Not all soy is the same

Try to buy soy closest to its natural form. Soybeans are the most natural but they take hours to cook and are not very versatile so you need to go a step down. The next best forms of soy are soy milk, tofu, soy flour, soy sauce, and miso (see below).

Soy milk can be used in cooking in the same way as cows' milk, and once mixed in with the other ingredients it is hard to taste the difference. Tofu (soy beancurd) can be used in stir-fries, soups, and also desserts. Soy flour can be very useful as it can be added to other flours to make cakes, pastries, etc.

Soy sauce, made from fermented soybeans, is fine as a flavoring but as you only need small amounts at a time it is not possible to obtain enough phytoestrogens. Miso is also made from fermented soybeans and is used as a paste to add to soups or stews.

The more processing that is done to the soy, the fewer phytoestrogens are in the food, as is the case with TVP (textured vegetable protein) which is made up into meat look-a-likes. If alcohol is used in the extraction process, all the plant estrogen value of the soy can be destroyed.

A high percentage of products containing soy are genetically modified. It is advisable to try to avoid such products where possible: check the label carefully and otherwise buy organic products. (For more details on GM foods, see page 36.)

How much phytoestrogen do you need?

As there are many foods which contain varying amounts of phytoestrogens, it is possible to have interesting and varied meals and still benefit. As a guideline, research has estimated that you should try to include 45mg of isoflavones per day in your diet. A typical serving (2 ounces of tofu or 1 pint of soy milk) will contain approximately 35 to 40 mg of isoflavones, so you do not need to eat masses of soy in order to achieve a good daily amount. That said, some Asian cultures can consume as much as 80mg a day in the form of miso soup, tofu, tempeh, etc., with no documented negative effects.

Phytoestrogens and the symptoms of menopause

There are numerous research papers on the beneficial effects of soy in reducing hot flashes. In one study the addition of only 1¾ ounces of soy flour a day reduced the number of hot flashes by 40 percent.[3] Another study reported in Obstetrics and Gynaecology in 1998 showed that after only two weeks of adding 2½ ounces of soy protein to the women's diet, they achieved a significant reduction in hot flashes compared to those women who were given a placebo (dummy mixture).[4]

The dramatic effect of phytoestrogens on hormone balance at menopause was shown in a study reported in the British Medical Journal. Women going through menopause had their normal diet supplemented with soy flour (1¾ ounces daily), linseeds (1 ounce daily) and red clover sprouts (a half-ounce daily). This change in diet reduced the amount of FSH (the hormone which rises at menopause) to pre-menopausal levels – thus putting the clock back naturally.

Although these phytoestrogen-rich foods made up only 10 percent of their total diet during the experiment, the effect of the phytoestrogens was strong enough to have a rapid and noticeable effect on the cells of the vagina, reducing vaginal dryness and irritation. These changes were detectable in just a few weeks and lasted for two months after the foods had been stopped, demonstrating that the consumption of phytoestrogens is crucial to fending off menopausal symptoms.[5]

Phytoestrogens and fibroids

Fibroids are non-cancerous growths which grow in or on the walls of the womb of some women and are very common as they get older. Many women will be unaware they have fibroids unless the fibroids cause heavy bleeding.

It is thought that fibroids grow due to an excess of estrogen, so, logically, as the body produces less estrogen at menopause they should start to shrink. Our bodies therefore have a natural way of dealing with fibroids, and adding more "bad" estrogens in the form of HRT can be detrimental. Try instead using natural methods, such as increasing your daily intake of soy, which is a source of "good" estrogens.

Soy will not only control any excess circulating estrogen but also its ability to stimulate the production of SHBG (sex hormone-binding globulin, see right), which binds onto estrogen, will be helpful in controlling the growth of fibroids.

Phytoestrogens and breast cancer

Breast cancer is predominantly estrogen-dependent. As we get older, our risk of breast cancer increases significantly (see

chart at right[6]), so anything that is going to lower that risk is to be welcomed. Increasing our intake of phytoestrogens is one method.

We have oestrogen receptors in the breasts which lock on to circulating estrogen. Phytoestrogens fit into these estrogen receptors in the breast and in so doing seem to block entry to the more carcinogenic estrogens, thus preventing cancer from developing.[7]

Soybeans have been found to contain at least five compounds believed to inhibit cancer. One of these is chemically similar to the drug tamoxifen, which is used to prevent estrogen-dependent breast cancer. Tamoxifen works in a similar way to phytoestrogens, locking onto the estrogen receptors and inhibiting cancer growth.

Another effect phytoestrogens have on the hormones is to stimulate the production of sex hormone-binding globulin (SHBG).[8] SHBG is a protein produced by the liver that binds sex hormones such as estrogen and testosterone in order to control how much of them are circulating in the blood at

Age	Risk of breast cancer
20	1 in 2,500
30	1 in 233
40	1 in 63
50	1 in 41
60	1 in 28
70	1 in 24
80	1 in 16
95	1 in 8

any one time. The fewer hormones there are circulating, the fewer are available to stimulate breast tissue and possibly cause cancer. This means that the phytoestrogens are able to lower the risk of hormone-related cancers such as breast cancer because they control the amount of free and active estradiol (the more carcinogenic estrogen).

Lastly, although we are bombarded by xenoestrogens in the environment (see page 11), studies have shown that genistein, the isoflavone in soy, can inhibit the growth and development of breast cancer cells induced by pesticides.[9]

Phytoestrogens and bones

Bone is in a continuous state of flux. It is constantly broken down and rebuilt through the body's biochemical processes. Bone loss results when the rate of renewal does not equal the rate of breakdown and can result in osteoporosis. Osteoporosis is a condition in which bones are porous – i.e., filled with tiny holes – and so become brittle, generating the risk of fractures.

HRT is often prescribed in order to protect women against osteoporosis. Unfortunately, many women are led to believe that HRT is the prime preventative measure without being told that osteoporosis could be prevented by other means such as nutrition and exercise without the risk of HRT side effects. And who knows if osteoporosis will happen anyway?

With all the scientific and medical interest in

soy, scientists have looked at the effect of soy on bone health. Genistein, one of the soy isoflavones, has been shown to inhibit the osteoclasts (cells which renew old bone by dissolving or reabsorbing it) and stimulate the osteoblasts (cells which replace the old bone with new).[10]
In a double-blind trial over two separate 12-week periods, bone density in postmenopausal women was increased by taking just 45mg per day of soy isoflavones.[11]

Our bones need calcium in order to remain strong and healthy. Research has shown that the more animal proteins we eat, the more calcium we excrete through our urine and therefore the greater risk of a hip fracture[12] (see High Protein Intake, page 31). Ironically, the table at right[13] also indicates that those countries that have the highest calcium intake also have the highest rate of hip fractures.

Although 98 percent of calcium is contained in our bones, it is not in fact the most important mineral in nutritional terms. Studies have shown that very often women who suffer from osteoporosis are not deficient in calcium, but are in fact deficient in other minerals such as magnesium and zinc.

Animal proteins are found in foods such as eggs, meat, chicken, and cheese. Studies have shown that when the same amount of calcium is taken with plant proteins such as soy, rather than animal proteins, the loss of calcium through the urine is lowered by 50 percent.[14]

In this way, isoflavone-rich foods could be helping the bones in two ways: firstly by

	Animal proteins (g per day)	Calcium intake (mg per day)	Hip fractures (100,000 persons)
South Africa	10	196	7
Singapore	25	389	22
Hong Kong	35	356	46
Spain	47	766	42
Great Britain	57	977	118
Denmark	58	960	165
Sweden	59	1104	188
Finland	60	1332	111
USA	72	973	145
New Zealand	78	1217	119

building up new bone and stopping too many old bone cells from being destroyed, and secondly by preventing excess urinary excretion of calcium.

Phytoestrogens and the heart

The rate of heart attacks in the West is much lower in women than men and by the age of 50 there is half as much risk for women as for men of suffering heart problems. It is not until the age of 75 that they have an equal risk to men. That said, it is still the biggest killer.

With the amount of research into cardio-vascular disease nowadays, scientists are clear about the strong link between heart problems and nutrition and have made us aware of how to reduce any risk through our diet by cutting down on saturated fats, etc. For many years, right up until 2002,

women were being recommended to take HRT in order to help prevent heart disease. In 1997 when I wrote the original Natural Alternatives to HRT book I stated that there was nothing to show that HRT would prevent heart disease.

But where did the idea come from that HRT could prevent heart problems? It started from a study[15] in the New England Journal of Medicine in 1985, with a follow-up in 1991, which tracked a group of nurses taking HRT over a period of years and compared them with another group not taking HRT. Those taking HRT were found to be less susceptible to heart attacks.

Unfortunately, the study was flawed in two ways: each nurse was fully aware of which group she belonged to, as were the scientists running the trial. In a properly controlled trial the people are split at random with one group being given a placebo (dummy pill). In this way no-one knows which pill they are taking. Nor are the scientists told which group has the drug. This is called a double-blind placebo controlled study: both parties are "blind" until it is over.

In the 1985 study of nurses, the women were assigned a group depending on whether they were already taking HRT or not. It is well known that there are certain contraindications and cautions against prescribing HRT, which include a history of thrombosis (blood clotting), liver disease, breast cancer, high blood pressure, breast cysts, fibroids, migraine, and endometriosis. Therefore none of the nurses with a history of thrombosis and high blood pressure would have been prescribed HRT in the first place and so would have been placed in the "not on HRT" group along with those nurses who had decided themselves not to take it. New research published in 2002 has shown that rather than lowering the risk of heart disease, HRT actually seems to increase it. As a result, the proposed eight year clinical trial run by the Women's Health Initiative in the USA had to be stopped because the evidence was showing that women on HRT had a 29 percent increased risk of heart disease.[16]

Phytoestrogens and cholesterol

Cholesterol is essential for life. It is manufactured in the liver and has a vital part to play in the structure of cells and the composition of certain hormones, particularly the sex hormones – oestrogens, progesterone, and testosterone.
Cholesterol is carried to the cells by low-density lipoprotein (LDL or "bad" cholesterol) and carried away to be excreted by high-density lipoprotein (HDL or "good" cholesterol). It is the balance of these two lipoproteins, far more than the total cholesterol level, that is so important to your health. If your LDL level is very high compared to your HDL level, cholesterol will be deposited in the artery walls, making them narrower and harder (atherosclerosis) but there is not enough HDL to remove it. The process is similar to the furring up of water pipes and can lead to heart disease. If you have a medical check-up it is definitely worth asking to have a lipid (fat) profile done which will give you all three measurements: total cholesterol, HDL, and LDL plus trigylcerides.

Remember that a lipid test needs to be done on an empty stomach, so organize the test to be performed in the morning and make sure you take nothing before you go except water. Ideally, your total cholesterol levels should be below 5.2 mmol per liter, with your LDL below 3.36 and HDL above 0.9. The ratio of your cholesterol to your HDL should not be more than 5 to 1.

What is the effect of soya on cholesterol?
Research has shown that a high level of cholesterol in the blood can be linked to the amount of saturated fat we eat. If your cholesterol level is high, dairy products and meat should be kept to a minimum. It is interesting that soy milk is naturally cholesterol-free. It is also rich in unsaturated fatty acids (see page 20). Studies have shown that eating soy decreases the LDL cholesterol and also the triglycerides.[17] It has also been found that the higher the person's initial cholesterol level the greater

is the effect of the soy. It is estimated that 25mg of soy protein a day can have this beneficial effect on cholesterol (tofu contains about ½ ounce of soy protein per 3½ ounces while two glasses of soy milk provide about 20 mg of soy protein).

How exactly the soy protein has this effect on cholesterol is not yet known, but several theories have been put forward:

✱ Excretion of bile: it is thought that soy increases fecal excretion of bile acids and in so doing pulls cholesterol from the body.
✱ Fiber effect: soy is a soluble fiber which will bind with some of the cholesterol and fat in the food you eat. As the fiber passes out unabsorbed, this also keeps fat levels under control.
✱ Antioxidant effect: it is now known that LDL becomes atherogenic when it has been oxidized. So antioxidants in our food (see page 23) can reduce narrowing of the arteries. The isoflavones genistein and daidzein which are present in soy both have antioxidant properties.[17]

Can you eat phytoestrogens and be on HRT?

Yes. In fact, it may be a definite advantage to eat phytoestrogens while taking HRT. HRT supplies you with the hormone estradiol (the more carcinogenic estrogen), so any measures that you can take to reduce its negative impact on the body are valuable. For example, phytoestrogens can act as estrogen receptor-antagonists in the breast, which may offer you some protection against breast cancer (see page 16).

Can eating phytoestrogens be used to help me come off HRT?

The question I am most asked is, "Should I just stop the HRT or should I come off it gradually?" You should talk to your doctor about your decision to come off HRT: the most informed doctors will tell you that a gradual weaning process is actually going to be easier on your body. Stopping HRT suddenly is similar to going "cold turkey" and there have been reports of "rebound" effects from the quick withdrawal of the hormones. The rebound effects can include tremendous hot flushes and seemingly worsened menopausal symptoms.

I believe that it is better to take three months to wean yourself slowly off HRT. Your doctor can help you do this by either gradually reducing the dose or, if you are using patches, leaving them longer before they are changed. If you still have a monthly bleed it is always important that it continues to happen regularly over the three-month period so that the womb lining is shed each time and doesn't build up. Your doctor will be able to advise you on this.

During that three-month period, you should start to introduce phytoestrogens into your diet. This will mean that when you stop the HRT you are cushioned by plant estrogens already circulating in your system, and any rebound effects should be minimal.

Phytoestrogens and the men in your life

Having established that phytoestrogens are beneficial for women's health, it is logical to ask how eating more phytoestrogen-rich foods such as legumes and soy will affect men. After all, this means an increase in oestrogen-like hormones in their bodies. In fact, it seems that phytoestrogens have a balancing effect on hormones in both men and women. Excess estrogen in men can trigger the overproduction of testosterone, and men with prostate cancer have higher levels of testosterone than men without the cancer. A diet full of phytoestrogens like soy can stimulate the production of SHGB (sex hormone-binding globulin) which controls circulating estrogen and testosterone, and so controls the cancer.

Studies have found that prostate cancer is approximately 30 times higher in Western men than in age-matched men in China and eight times that in Japan.[19] The scientists first thought that it was the Western men's higher intake of animal fats that was causing the cancer, but further research showed that it is the phytoestrogens that are the reason for a lower cancer rate in Asian men. Japanese men who ate tofu more than five times a week had half the risk of prostate cancer compared with Japanese men who ate tofu less than once a week. Another study showed that when Chinese men were compared against Caucasian men in the UK, isoflavonoid levels in prostatic fluid were seven times higher in the Chinese men.[20]

Essential fatty acids (EFAs)

It is important to understand that some fats are vital to health, while others are not. We have to learn to distinguish between them, not simply to cut them out of our diet altogether. Most foods will contain varying amounts of saturated, monounsaturated, and poly-unsaturated fats. It is the predominance of one type of fat over another that makes a difference to your health.

Essential fatty acids are literally essential for your health, and are the next most important group of foods to be included at menopause after phytoestrogens. Essential fats "oil" the body by lubricating the joints, skin, and vagina as well as performing other functions. Because of the recurring message that fat is "bad," most of us will have reduced the amount of fat in our diets, to the point where some women are living on completely fat-free diets. However, it is important to differentiate between the

---

Phytoestrogens summary

* Provides estrogen in plant form
* Controls menopausal symptoms
* Protects against breast and womb cancer, and also prostate cancer
* Helps to maintain a healthy heart and lower cholesterol
* Prevents osteoporosis

types of fats. Without sufficient EFAs, the body will start to send out warnings that there is a deficiency of essential fats. The problem is that these warnings can be quite subtle at first. Signs could include dry skin, lifeless hair, cracked nails, fatigue, depression, dry eyes, lack of motivation, aching joints, difficulty in losing weight, forgetfulness, breast pain – all symptoms which could be "blamed" on menopause.

If a deficiency in EFAs is not corrected, the problems can become more serious and can include heart disease, cancer, arthritis, and depression. Unfortunately, all too often such illnesses are viewed as part of the degenerative process of getting older – "just one of those things."

Polyunsaturated fats

These are the fats that are essential for health. They are found in nuts, seeds, oily fish, and some vegetables.

The essential oils in nuts and seeds are from the Omega 6 family of oils which includes evening primrose, starflower and borage oil. The best of these for eating on a regular basis are sesame, walnut, sunflower, and soy. These essential fatty acids help prevent blood clots and keep the blood thin. They can also reduce inflammation and pain in the joints and so are vital in preventing arthritis. Interestingly, both sesame and soy are also classed as sources of phytoestrogens (see page 15).

The Omega 3 family of oils is found in oily fish and is also present to some extent in pumpkin seeds, walnuts, and dark green vegetables. These oils can help lower blood

pressure, reduce the risk of heart disease, soften the skin, increase immune function, increase metabolic rate, improve energy levels, as well as alleviate eczema.

Oily fish include mackerel, tuna, sardines, herrings, and salmon. A small portion of salmon (4 ounces) can contain up to 3,600 mg of Omega 3 fatty acids, while the same size piece of cod will contain only 300mg. A small portion of fish can supply us with almost half of our protein requirements for a day as well as providing us with good levels of B12 and iodine, which is essential for the healthy function of the thyroid and metabolism.

Fish oils are also extremely useful in the treatment of psoriasis. A number of clinical trials have shown significant improvements in patients when they were given a half-ounce of EPA (epicosapentaenoic acid) – about the same as eating 5 ounces of mackerel – in their diet.[21] As these oils act as a kind of lubricant it is clear that they are especially important for us at menopause, when our skin and vaginal tissues can become drier.

Other studies have shown that eating one portion of oily fish a day can have a dramatic positive effect on rheumatoid arthritis.[22] Polyunsaturated fish oils seem to stop the inflammatory response in the joints and hence alleviate the pain. Many of the women I see complain of aching and stiff joints at menopause, and I usually recommend that they increase their intake of these fish oils.

There can be a tendency for women to gain weight at menopause, which is often the body's protective mechanism to

increase the amount of estrogen circulating in the bloodstream by producing it from your fat cells. This happens when your ovaries slow down their estrogen production.

It is excess weight gain that is the problem and this comes about through changes in your metabolism. Essential Omega 3 oils can increase metabolic rate which means that you will burn up more fat and store less fat (for further help with natural weight loss see my book *Natural Alternatives to Dieting*).

A lot of weight problems can simply be due to water retention. Omega 3 oils help your body to produce a hormone-like regulating substance (prostaglandin) which enables your kidneys to eliminate excess water. These prostaglandins also help to lower blood pressure and decrease inflammation in the joints.

Foods Containing EFAs
✱ Nuts (e.g., almonds, brazils, walnuts)
✱ Seeds (e.g., sunflower, pumpkin, sesame, flax seeds)
✱ Oily fish (e.g., mackerel, sardines)

Monounsaturated fats

Unlike polyunsaturated fats, mono-unsaturated fats are not essential for health, but they do have other health benefits. Olive oil contains mainly monounsaturated fats and has been found to lower LDL ("bad" cholesterol) and raise HDL ("good" cholesterol), which is one of the factors that contribute to the low rate of heart disease in the Mediterranean.

Olive oil has been used for many years with lemon juice to act as a liver cleanse (see my book *The Natural Alternatives to HRT*). Use mainly olive oil for cooking rather than a polyunsaturated oil like sunflower oil because there is less chance of damaging the oil and creating free radicals (see page 25).

Quality of oils

Quality makes a great difference to the beneficial effects of an oil. Look for cold-pressed unrefined organic oils and extra virgin organic olive oil. Extra virgin olive oil is unrefined, and is made traditionally from whole, ripe, undamaged olives. The oil is extracted without heat. Extra virgin olive oil is generally the only oil you can buy in supermarkets that is not refined. Some supermarkets will also have organic extra virgin olive oil. Most other supermarket oils such as sunflower are refined in order to obtain the maximum amount of oil from each batch. This destroys the quality of the oil and the nutritional content. Even more worryingly, the refining process – often at temperatures above 320°F – can increase the risk of cell mutation when consumed.

All oils should be kept in the cold and away from sunlight. Exposing the oil to light or heat – e.g., leaving the bottle on a windowsill or heating the oil to high temperatures – can cause oxidation. This makes the oil susceptible to attack by free radicals (see page 23). These free radicals have been linked to cancer and premature aging.

Heating nuts and seeds to high temperatures, by roasting them for example, can also damage the essential oils in them, so

it is better to sprinkle them raw onto salads and vegetables. Otherwise make sure that you only toast them very lightly.

Flax seed

These seeds have been given a special mention as they can be highly beneficial at menopause.

Flax oil is more widely known for oiling cricket bats and making linen and yet it is also classed as a "miracle" food which we have tended to overlook, and is similar to soy with its range of benefits. The Latin name for flax seed is *Linum usitatissimum*, with the second part meaning "most useful," which you will see it is.

Flax seeds are unusual in that they contain not only the Omega 6 oils that other seeds contain but they also contain good quantities of Omega 3 oils. (See page 20 for details on their benefits.)

Flax seeds are rich in phytoestrogens, but while soy contains isoflavones, flax seeds contain lignans, which is a different class of phytoestrogen. Lignans are believed to carry the same benefits as isoflavones (see page 15), but are also anti-viral, anti-fungal, and anti-bacterial. A good regular intake of lignans has also been associated with lower incidence of cancer of the breast, ovaries, uterus, prostate, and colon.[23]

Flax seed is by far the best source of lignans: in fact, it is 100 times richer than the next in line, wheat bran. I would not recommend eating wheat bran at all in your diet because it is a refined food (see page 33). If you are troubled by constipation, try flax seeds instead of bran. They work like roughage to stimulate the bowel and make motions more comfortable. For constipation, soak a tablespoon of flax seeds in water and swallow at breakfast. Otherwise, put some flax seeds in a grinder and eat them half cracked sprinkled on food (their nutrients are more easily absorbed if they are broken up).

How much flax seed do you need?
One tablespoon of flax seeds is estimated to be the equivalent of one portion of soy – i.e., two ounces tofu or soy flour, or one pint soy milk. You can effectively use them interchangeably. I would suggest that if you have menopausal symptoms you use a combination of different phytoestrogens to obtain the best effect. This will of course also give you more variety and choice in your diet.

In a study in the British Medical Journal, a group of postmenopausal women were asked to change just 10 percent of their diet to include phytoestrogens. The amount of flax seed given per day was about two tablespoons, with soy and red clover making up the rest of the 10 percent. Before the study the women showed signs of oestrogen deficiency, especially in the vagina, with lack of secretions and a feeling of tightness. Within six weeks they reported significant changes: their vaginas became moist and there was a "plumping up" of the vaginal tissues.

How do you use flax seed?
Flax seeds are small (just bigger than sesame seeds) so it is easy to mix them with other foods. Flax seeds are excellent mixed into yogurt – either organic plain live yogurt or soy yogurt – for an extra source of phytoestrogens. The golden and brown flax seeds have the same qualities; the golden ones just look better!

Flaxseed oil can be used in any recipe where you would use uncooked oil, such as salad dressings, but it is unsuitable for frying. In recipes where you normally might use olive oil only, e.g., hummus, try combining half flaxseed oil and half olive oil. Flaxseed oil is also excellent drizzled on roasted vegetables or jacket potatoes.

The Shopping and Cooking Tips section of the book suggests a delicious seed mix (see page 42) which will give you both the phytoestrogen benefits and excellent levels of essential fatty acids.

Antioxidants

Ageing
Few of us welcome the physical changes that come with getting older, but although we can't turn back the clock it is possible to slow it down – naturally.

HRT is often touted as the "fountain of youth," as Dr Robert Wilson, a New York gynecologist, wrote in his book famously called *Feminine Forever* (1996). He declared that without this elixir women are "unstable, oestrogen-starved... a misery to themselves and everyone else, causing, at the extreme, alcoholism, drug addiction, divorce, and broken homes"! However, HRT is by no means the only way of releasing us from this "misery": food is our weapon, particularly when it contains antioxidants (see right).

An experiment which started in 1912 involved live chicken cells being fed certain nutrients every day. The cells accordingly would divide and form new cells, and any excess cells died off regularly.
The experiment lasted 34 years and was only stopped when the biologist heading the program died.[24] It was realized that in this "ideal" situation these cells could continue indefinitely; in other words, be immortal.

In theory, therefore, if we only put into our systems the right quality and quantity of the fuel that it needs, lived in a sterile environment (without pollutants), and eliminated all waste products, we would never age. Time would pass but the body would always be able to rejuvenate itself.

This, however, is not how we live. It is now thought that each cell is programmed to divide a certain number of times (50) before they start to look "old," suggesting that we have a genetic clock inside us.

Combating free radicals

Oxygen is the basis of all plant and animal life and is vital for our survival. Yet it is also chemically reactive and can therefore be highly dangerous. During normal biochemical reactions oxygen can become unstable, resulting in the "oxidation" of other molecules, which in turn generates free radicals. Free radicals are also triggered by our environment, which has been made so much more harmful in recent decades by pollution, smoke, and UV rays.

It is these free radicals that have been linked to premature aging, cancer, and coronary heart disease as well as to the brown patches on the skin of some elderly people. Free radicals speed up the aging process by destroying healthy cells and attacking collagen, the "cement" that holds cells together which is the primary organic constituent of bone, cartilage, and connective tissue like skin. They can attack the DNA in the nucleus of a cell, causing cell mutation and cancer. Apart from the normal biochemical processes in the body, other sources of free radicals are fried or barbecued food, radiation, exhaust fumes, and smoking.

Fortunately, nature provides us with protection against free radicals in the form of antioxidants. Antioxidants are extremely important because they can disarm free radicals. Our bodies produce some antioxidants naturally, but in the polluted society in which we live we need more antioxidants than our bodies can manufacture, so the best solution is to eat them.

In order to get a good supply of antioxidants you need to eat a wide variety of fruits and vegetables, preferably organic. Try to avoid peeling them as the skin can

Essential fats summary

* Maintain a healthy heart
* Minimize aching and stiff joints
* Prevent degenerative diseases like arthritis
* Protect against cancer
* Control weight naturally
* Bring good mental health
* Control menopausal symptoms

Sources of antioxidants

Vitamin A	Orange and yellow fruits and vegetables, e.g., carrots and pumpkins
Vitamin C	Fruits (particularly citrus), green leafy vegetables such as broccoli, cauliflower, berries, potatoes, and sweet potatoes
Vitamin E	Nuts, avocados, seeds, vegetable oils, and oily fish
Selenium	Brazil nuts, tuna, cabbage
Zinc	Pumpkin and sunflower seeds, fish, almonds

contain valuable nutrients and antioxidants. This is where the "French Paradox" comes in. Why do the French have such a low rate of heart disease (only 30 percent of ours) and yet tend to eat more saturated fat than we do? Scientists found that it was wine, especially red wine, that was protecting the French. Unfortunately the benefits have nothing to do with the alcohol but the grapes themselves.

Grapes contain an antioxidant called resveratrol which decreases the "stickiness" of the blood platelets and keeps blood vessels from narrowing.[25] This resveratrol is mainly contained in the skin of grapes, which is why red wine seems to be more effective than white. (Red wine is made from the whole grapes including the skin and seeds whereas white wine is only made from the fleshy bit.) So the message here is to forget the glass of red wine and just eat a bunch of grapes – either black or white – skin included.

Luckily, antioxidants are found in many foods that are easy and enjoyable to eat on a regular basis and are included in plentiful supply in this book's recipes. Foods containing the vitamins C, E, and beta-carotene (the plant form of vitamin A) all have antioxidant properties, as do the minerals selenium and zinc. The Omega 3 oils in oily fish and linseeds can also mop up free radicals. Some important plant chemicals are also powerful antioxidants, such as lycopene (found in tomatoes), bioflavonoids (found in citrus fruits), and proanthocyanidins (found in berries, grapes, and green tea).

Beta-carotene (vitamin A)
Beta-carotene is one of the most important antioxidants that we can eat.
It is found predominantly in orange and yellow vegetables and fruits such as sweet potatoes, peaches, and papayas. Carrots and pumpkins are also excellent sources of beta-carotene: the old wives' tale that states that carrots enable you to see better in the dark is actually backed up by science (you've never seen a rabbit wearing glasses, have you?). Indeed, a deficiency of vitamin A can cause "night blindness."

Green vegetables are also rich in beta-carotene, including watercress, kale, and broccoli.

Lycopene
The carotene lycopene, found primarily in tomatoes but also present in red fruits and red peppers, may have a preventative effect against cancer, heart disease, and degenerative eye conditions. However, scientists have discovered that when tomatoes are eaten raw, very little lycopene is absorbed into the bloodstream. It seems that the antioxidant is more readily absorbed when the tomatoes are cooked in oil, such as extra virgin olive oil.

This helps to explain why the Mediterranean diet is associated with a lower risk of heart disease and certain cancers. Studies show that lycopene in its natural form helps prevent the build-up of the cholesterol LDL (see page 18). In addition, when lycopene was added to cancer cell cultures, the lycopene inhibited their growth.[26]

Vitamin C
Nearly all animals naturally make vitamin C in their bodies except us, guinea pigs, fruit-eating bats, primates, the red-vented bulbul bird, and the teleost fish! Most animals will produce around 3,000 to 16,000mg per day, whereas we have to get it all from our diet.

Vitamin C is water-soluble and excreted within two or three hours, so it is important to have adequate amounts regularly. It is valuable in preventing premature aging and cancer as well as having an extremely important part to play in preventing osteoporosis, like flavonoids (see below).

Vitamin E
This important vitamin is good for the skin and helps to keep the blood from clotting inappropriately – which is especially important at menopause when one of our biggest risks is heart disease. Vitamin E can also have a direct effect on cholesterol by protecting us from the damage wrought by LDL, the "bad" cholesterol (see page 18).

Other antioxidants: flavonoids
The vitamins and minerals mentioned above are essential nutrients, necessary to maintain our bodily functions. They are antioxidants as well as many other things; they are involved in so many different processes in the body. There is another group of antioxidants which is often classed as "semi-essential" nutrients because, although we do not need them to live, they can provide enormous health benefits. This group is called the flavonoids, of which more than 4,000 compounds have been characterized. Two of them are especially

important at menopause: bioflavonoids and proanthocyanidins.

Bioflavonoids

These antioxidants are very closely associated with vitamin C and are found in citrus fruits. They are important in controlling inflammation and allergies[27] and are excellent at strengthening capillaries which can become more fragile as we get older, leading to bruising at the slightest knock.[28] Fragile capillaries can also be a reason for heavy periods: increasing the intake of vitamin C and bioflavonoids has been found to be helpful.[29] Periods can become heavier at menopause, which may be due to changes in blood vessels but

may also be due to fibroids (see page 16). Bioflavonoids also help to preserve the collagen matrix which can so easily be damaged by free radicals.[30] Collagen is important for the growth and repair of cells, gums, blood vessels, and teeth and makes up about 90 percent of bones. It is therefore vital that women eat lots of bioflavonoids as they near menopause in order to ward off osteoporosis.

Collagen also helps to preserve the elasticity of the skin. The walls of the vagina become thinner and drier at menopause due to changes in estrogen. If the walls of the vagina become less elastic they will not be able to stretch comfortably to accommodate an erect penis, so making intercourse painful.

Eating decent quantities of bioflavonoids and vitamin C can help enormously in preserving the collagen inside the vagina – and your sex life. It can also help retain the elasticity in the urinary tract and so prevent leakage or stress incontinence, which is common in menopausal women.

Proanthocyanidins

These flavonoids give the deep color to many berries such as blackberries, blueberries, raspberries, etc. They are excellent "free radical scavengers" and, like bioflavonoids, help to preserve the integrity of the capillaries and so lessen varicose veins. With their powerful antioxidant properties, they play a major part in the prevention of heart disease and strokes.

Proanthocyanidins also have a place in preventing osteoporosis because they strengthen the collagen matrix and stop the destruction of collagen. Studies have also

shown the benefits of these antioxidants on visual function, which is something that can deteriorate as we reach menopause.

Potassium

Potassium is vital for the healthy functioning of the heart. A study published in *The Lancet* (UK) in September 1999 showed that women with higher blood pressure had a greater and faster loss of bone minerals. The head of the research team from St. George's Medical School in London advised such women to eat more potassium, which is present in dandelions as well as in fruits and vegetables, such as celery, apricots, dates, and figs.

Fiber

There are two main types of fiber: soluble and insoluble fiber. Insoluble fiber (like cellulose) is found in whole grains and vegetables while soluble fiber is found in fruit, oats, and beans.

Fiber is known for its action on the bowel, and is beneficial for problems like constipation. It binds water and increases the bulk of stools so that they are easier to eliminate from the body. To correct constipation you need to increase your intake of insoluble fiber, which can also help reduce diseases of the colon including colon cancer and diverticulitis.

Fiber also prevents the putrefaction of food which can result if food stays in the bowel too long. Putrefying food will ferment, causing a build-up of gas which leads to bloating and flatulence. Chronic constipation has been linked to breast cancer. This is due to the fact that if toxic waste products and "old" hormones are not expelled efficiently they can end up stored in the body's fatty tissue, including the breasts. The amount of fiber in your diet determines how much estrogen you store and how much you excrete, so it is very important at menopause. Soluble fiber, contained in foods like soy, oats, and lentils, binds oestrogen so that it is excreted more efficiently.

Our greatest killer is cardiovascular disease (roughly 50 percent of women will die of heart disease in the US, more than twice as many as from all forms of cancer, including breast cancer), and the risk increases as we get older. It is therefore very important that we keep our hearts healthy at menopause. Soluble fiber binds with some of the cholesterol and fat in the food you eat. As the fiber passes out unabsorbed, it also keeps fat levels under control. Fiber can be useful in weight management in other ways: it aids digestion, increases your feeling of fullness, and removes toxins from the body. By making you feel full it helps you to feel more satisfied with what you have eaten and lessens the tendency to overeat.

Lignans, the phytoestrogens, are also a fiber-like substance (see page 15). Two of the best-known lignans are linseed and wheat bran. To alleviate any bowel problems I advise you use linseeds rather than wheat bran; that way you will enjoy both the benefits from the phytoestrogens as well as the fiber from the same food. Wheat bran should not be eaten except when it is contained naturally in food, e.g., whole-wheat bread. Phytates, which are substances within the bran, have a binding effect on certain minerals – e.g., iron,

---

Antioxidants summary

* Anti-aging
* Protect against cancer
* Prevent osteoporosis
* Maintain a healthy heart
* Protect skin and vaginal tissues
* Bring optimum health
* Alleviate menopausal symptoms

---

calcium, zinc, and magnesium – making them harder to be absorbed. Raw grain contains phytates, so soak granola before eating to break them down.

Special foods

Three other groups of foods need a mention because they contain specific substances which can be very helpful at menopause.

Cruciferous vegetables
As children, most of us have probably been told to "eat our greens" and there are definite reasons why we should, especially at menopause. As we get older our risk of developing breast cancer increases. Cruciferous vegetables like cabbage, broccoli, and Brussels sprouts help guard against estrogen-dependent cancers. They contain the compound indol-3-carbinol which changes the way estrogen is metabolized in the body by speeding up its elimination, thus making it less dangerous.

Cauliflowers also contain sulphurous compounds that may help to protect against colon cancer. We tend to think of fruit in connection with vitamin C, but cauliflowers can in fact contain more than the recommended daily intake of vitamin C in one helping than in an orange. Cabbages are also a good source of vitamins C, E, and K. Both vitamins C and E are antioxidants (see page 23) and so are excellent as anti-cancer and anti-aging agents. Vitamin K is manufactured from bacteria in our intestines and is vital for normal blood clotting. It is also essential for proper bone formation. Vitamin K is needed to synthesize osteocalcin, a unique protein found in large amounts in bone. Blood levels of vitamin K have been found to be up to 35 percent lower in people with osteoporosis.[31] Cabbage is one of the richest sources of vitamin K, but other leafy vegetables like broccoli and Brussels sprouts also contain good levels.

Broccoli is a wonderful vegetable for the health, with good amounts of vitamin C and beta-carotene – both powerful antioxidants helpful for anti-aging and cancer protection. The darker the florets, the more of these two nutrients the vegetable contains.

The allium family
The allium family includes garlic, onions, leeks, and scallions. A study reported in the scientific journal Nature in September 1999 showed that onions, amongst a few other vegetables, could prevent osteoporosis. The scientists were unsure which exact elements in the onions make the difference, but rats fed on onions over a period of four weeks developed thicker and stronger bones. The experiment clearly needs to be repeated on humans before any real conclusions are made.

Garlic, one of the other vegetables from the study found to be beneficial, also contains cancer-inhibiting properties. Garlic's sulphur compounds increase the activity of macrophages and T-lymphocytes, two components of the immune system that destroy tumor cells. Around 1,500 B.C., the Egyptians documented the use of garlic for headaches and throat problems, and garlic is also mentioned in the literature of the ancient Greeks and Romans. Garlic has also been found to increase HDL ("good" cholesterol) levels, so lowering blood cholesterol and triglycerides (circulating fat in the body).[32] Although garlic is a wonderful remedy for many health problems, some people hesitate to eat it because of its odor. Remember that you can chew parsley after eating it to freshen your breath.

Seaweeds

Seaweed is low in calories and has a very good mineral content including the trace minerals zinc, manganese, chromium, selenium, and cobalt, and the macro minerals calcium, magnesium, iron, and iodine. Iodine is essential for the healthy functioning of the thyroid gland which regulates metabolism. Unfortunately, the metabolism often becomes sluggish at menopause, so seaweed is particularly useful at this time. Scientific studies have shown that the consumption of seaweed can also have anti-cancer benefits[33] and can reduce cholesterol and improve fat metabolism.[34]

Sources of fiber

* Fresh fruit and vegetables, both cooked and raw
* Whole grains, e.g., brown rice, whole-wheat bread, wholegrain crackers, whole-wheat pasta
* Nuts and seeds
* Beans, e.g., soy, lentils

Fiber summary

* Prevents cancer
* Maintains a healthy heart
* Controls weight naturally
* Prevents constipation and flatulence
* Controls estrogen levels

what you don't need during menopause

what you don't need during menopause

We've talked about foods that are beneficial to eat during menopause. These are simple to include on a daily basis, as you'll see from the recipes that follow. But it is also important to discuss which elements of your diet can actually make menopause worse and increase your chances of getting osteoporosis or heart problems. Some of the foods and drinks mentioned affect us all while some are peculiar to each woman.

With hot flashes, for example, look for your "triggers." Is there something you eat or drink that will suddenly bring on a hot flash? The common triggers are caffeinated drinks such as coffee, red wine, spicy foods, and hot drinks (due to the temperature). Recently, one patient simply avoided alcohol for a week and completely eliminated her hot flashes. It is not usual for hot flashes to disappear totally by cutting out one item, but it worked for her. She then had the hard task of weighing up whether she preferred the hot flashes or the red wine!

I would encourage experimenting and maybe keeping a small diary to note when the hot flashes occur to ascertain if they are connected with anything you have just eaten or drunk. Effects can become evident within half an hour of eating or drinking the "villain."

It goes without saying that it is no good planning healthy meals, including phytoestrogens and antioxidants in your meals, if you are also eating foods that disrupt your hormone balance, leech calcium from your bones, and are detrimental to your general well-being. You will be fighting a losing battle.

This must seem like the bad news section of the book – reducing sugar, tea, and coffee, etc. But when you look at the amount of foods that are valuable at menopause you'll see that in comparison there are only a few that you should reduce or eliminate. If you eat fairly well at home and then go on holiday or are invited out to dinner, the odd "blip" will not make too much difference. Just make sure that the foundation of your food at home is good.

High protein intake

We need protein. It is the basic building block for all our cells and bones as well as our hair, skin, and nails. It is made from 25 amino acids, eight of which are called "essential" because we must get them from our diet, while the other 17 can be made in the body. However, an excess of protein can generate problems including kidney stones and Crohn's disease.

Protein causes an acidic reaction in the body and it is calcium's role in the body to act as a neutralizer. When you eat too much protein, your own reserves of calcium from your bones and teeth are called up to correct the imbalance. The calcium is then eliminated from the body through your urine. It is estimated that for every extra half-ounce of protein that you eat, 100mg of calcium is lost in your urine.

In 1996, scientists at the Harvard School of Public Health investigated ideal quantities of protein in our diet. They found that women who ate more than 3½ ounces of animal protein a day had an increased risk of forearm fractures compared with women who ate less than 2¾ ounces per day.

An average portion of bacon is 1¾ ounces while just two pork sausages weigh approximately 3½ ounces, which makes you realize quite how easy it is to eat far too much protein.

Notably, the same study found that for those women who ate vegetable rather than animal protein there was no increased risk of fractures. (Tofu, for instance, is classed as a vegetable protein.)

The year after this study the British Government's Department of Health Committee on Medical Aspects of Food and Nutrition Policy (COMA) took the rare step of publishing a report entitled "Nutritional Aspects of the Development of Cancer," which indicated a possible link between the consumption of red meat (an animal protein) and bowel cancer. It suggested that any intake at or above the current average of around 3¼ ounces per day should be reduced.

Consumption of red meat can therefore not only increase the risk of osteoporosis but also increase the likelihood of bowel cancer. My recommendation would be to eliminate it altogether. You'll see from the recipes in this book that you can live quite easily and eat extremely well without red meat in your diet. Instead, you could obtain your animal protein from fish and the occasional egg and dairy products (yogurt is the healthiest).

It was previously thought that vegetable proteins were "incomplete" as only the animal proteins contain all the essential amino acids. This has been disproved by the discovery that the combination of a variety of vegetables provides all the amino acids we need. Therefore it is perfectly possible to be a vegetarian and obtain sufficient quantities of protein. A 150-pound person needs no more than 1½ ounces of protein a day.

Dairy foods

Dairy products are constantly the subject of nutritional advice, often conflicting. You

---

Sources of animal protein

* Red meat, poultry, fish, eggs, dairy products, etc

Sources of vegetable protein

* Cereals, e.g. wheat, oats, rice
* Pulses, e.g. soy, lentils
* Nuts

---

have probably been told that you should eat them sparingly because of their high saturated fat content, and yet you need them for their calcium content. However, as they are an animal protein they could make you excrete more calcium than your body takes in.

Dairy products such as cheese, milk, and cream should be used in small amounts as they contain the protein casein. Casein is 300 times higher in cows' milk than it is in human milk. Many people believe that our systems were not really designed to cope with cows' milk. Researchers have found that breast-fed babies absorb more calcium from their mother's milk than from cows' milk despite the fact that cows' milk contains four times the amount of calcium.

An added problem is that cows are fed antibiotics to speed up their growth. A generation ago an individual cow would produce approximately two gallons of milk per day; now it yields 12 gallons per day. Because of the increasing tampering with nature, I would advise that you make sure that the dairy products you buy are organic.

At menopause you are also trying to protect your heart, so it is important to keep the saturated fat content of your diet low (see right). Dairy foods are high in saturated fat, so they should be eaten in moderation.

With low-fat dairy products, the protein content of that food will be higher as part of the fat will have been removed. However, as explained above, the higher the protein content the more calcium you will lose and the greater risk to your bones. So although your heart may benefit by eating low-fat products, your bones will not! Ultimately it is much better to buy dairy foods the way that nature intended, e.g., full-fat milk rather than skimmed, and to eat them in moderation.

Lastly, you should realize that you are not dependent on dairy foods to obtain calcium. Indeed, many other foods contain more easily absorbable forms of calcium. Sesame seeds are high in calcium, as are some nuts. Almonds, for instance, contain 304mg of calcium in 3½ ounces. Broccoli is also high in calcium, with 200mg in 3½ ounces.

Saturated fats

You do not need saturated fats, which come from animals and are contained in foods such as meat, eggs, and dairy products such as cheese, etc. These are hard fats – fats which are solid at room temperature, and therefore the most saturated.

Saturated fats can be detrimental to your health by increasing the risk of athero-sclerosis, where deposits of fatty materials are laid down in the arteries. They can also make it more difficult for your body to get the benefits of the essential fats that you eat. Additionally, saturated fat can be mucus-forming and cause problems with catarrh, runny noses (rhinitis), and skin problems such as eczema.

Trans fats

Trans fats (hydrogenated fats) are produced from polyunsaturated oils, as used in margarines. This process involves the hydrogenation of the oil to make it into a solid mass. It is best to avoid hydrogenated fats as they can increase cholesterol and the risk of atherosclerosis, lower HDL (the "good" cholesterol) and block the body's assimilation of essential fatty acids, making a deficiency more problematic.

Refined foods

Sugar and white flour are refined foods, which means that the fiber and most of the vitamins, minerals, and trace elements have been stripped away. Sugar is nothing but "empty calories;" it contains no nutritional value. Moreover, in order to digest refined foods your body has to use its own vitamins and minerals, so depleting its own stores. Foods containing white flour include cakes, cookies, breads, and pastries. As far as possible it is advisable to avoid such foods.

Sugar

You will notice that none of the recipes here contains sugar. Like protein, sugar causes you to excrete more calcium through your urine because it is acidic. So even if you were following an excellent diet for menopause, if you included sugary foods you would reduce the benefits of the good foods.

Sugar carries another negative effect at menopause. When you eat sugar (and foods containing white flour), digestion is fast and glucose enters the body rapidly. Your blood glucose levels rise quickly but are then followed by a sharp drop. This drop is called hypoglycemia, or low blood sugar, and can make you feel tired, irritable, light-headed, and have palpitations. When blood glucose levels fall, your body releases the hormone adrenaline from the adrenal glands and the pancreas produces glucagon. Glucagon helps to bring your blood glucose levels up again.

The problem with this is that the adrenal glands are having to work overtime, releasing adrenaline every time your blood sugar drops. At menopause it is especially important that your adrenal glands are working at their optimum because it becomes their job to produce a form of estrogen while your ovaries start to produce less. If your adrenal glands become exhausted they will not be able to provide this protection in the form of extra estrogen.

Thirdly, it is also well known that it is sugar that makes you fat. Essentially what happens is that the more sugar you eat, the more insulin is released. Every time you eat, your body has the choice of either burning that food off as energy or storing it as fat. When insulin is released more of your food is converted into fat and previously stored fat is not broken down.

However much you should avoid sugar, don't substitute it with artificial sweeteners. This merely introduces an alien chemical which the body has to deal with. You are trying to keep your body balanced at menopause, and nobody really knows yet what havoc these chemicals can cause.

Food can still taste sweet and yet not contain sugar. In some of the recipes that follow, other forms of natural sweetener are used in moderation, such as maple syrup. You will soon find that as you reduce your usual intake of sugar, you will start to taste the sweetness in foods like carrots and baked parsnips. And if you haven't eaten sugar for a while and then try some, it can taste too sweet and you won't actually like it. Honestly!

Bran

Like sugar, bran is usually sold as a refined food so I would not suggest you include it in your diet. Bran should only be eaten the way nature intended – as a grain in its whole state – or when it is contained naturally within the food, e.g., whole-wheat bread (wheat bran) or porridge oats (oat bran). If you suffer from constipation, try flax seeds (see pages 22–23) instead.

Soft drinks

Carbonated soft drinks should be eliminated from your diet. They contain high amounts of phosphorus which helps to leech calcium out of your bones. Nowadays it is very easy to consume far too much phosphorus since it is found in most junk foods, including instant soups and puddings as well as carbonated drinks.

Concentrated fruit syrups do not contain phosphorus, but are equally bad for the health because of the amount of sugar they contain.

Instead, use pure unsweetened fruit juice and avoid any that say "fruit drink" on the label as more often than not something else has been added. Liven up fruit juice with sparkling water and for a treat try Appletizer, Aqua Libra, and Amé. These are natural and make an effective alcohol substitute. You can also find delicious "real" lemonade which is free from sugar, preservatives, and artificial colors and flavors.

Tea and coffee

What is wrong with tea and coffee? They both contain caffeine, although tea contains less than coffee. It has been shown that the more caffeine that is drunk the more calcium is lost. Like protein, caffeine causes an acid reaction, so that calcium is taken from your bones to neutralize the acid. Accordingly, drinking more than two cups of coffee (or four cups of tea) a day can increase the risk of hip fractures.[1]

Furthermore, both tea and coffee act as diuretics and so can flush out many vital nutrients and trace elements. There are also substances in caffeinated drinks and foods (e.g., chocolate) called methylxanthines which have been linked to a benign breast disease called fibrocystic disease.

This condition makes the breasts feel very uncomfortable, tender, and lumpy in the week or two weeks before a period. As you lead up to menopause this condition can worsen, making it difficult to sleep, lie on your stomach, or even be hugged. The problem can often be eliminated by cutting out coffee, chocolate, cola drinks, cocoa and tea – a simple solution.

Like sugar, both tea and coffee act as stimulants and so place a strain on the adrenal glands by making them pump out more adrenaline. It is important not to overwork your adrenal glands, especially at menopause when the glands manufacture estrogen to compensate for the dwindling production by the ovaries.

Black tea also contains tannin which binds important minerals and prevents their absorption in the digestive tract. So it is counterproductive to eat a good meal full of phytoestrogens and healthy foods and drink a cup of tea at the same time.

Alternatives for tea and coffee

Instead of ordinary black tea try herb teas, fruit teas, Rooibos (caffeine-free South African tea), green tea (in moderation because it contains caffeine) and Japanese twig (bancha) tea.

As well as the best-known herb teas – peppermint (for digestion) and camomile (relaxing) – there are a number of other herb teas which can be extremely helpful at menopause. Nettle tea contains good amounts of calcium and can also help to strengthen the adrenal glands, which is valuable at menopause when we need the extra estrogen from the adrenal glands (see page 10). Nettle tea is also helpful in counteracting hot flashes, as is sage tea.

Green tea (*Camellia sinensis*) is an interesting drink. Both green and "ordinary" black tea come from the same plant but in green tea the leaves are not fermented. Although green tea contains a small amount of caffeine, it also contains polyphenols which have been credited for the health benefits of the tea. Green tea can help to reduce estrogen by stopping estrogen from gaining access to the estrogen receptors in estrogen-sensitive tumors.[2] As well as the prevention of breast cancer, polyphenols have been found to lessen the risk of other cancers and also to reduce the risk of heart disease by lowering cholesterol. Both black and green teas contain bioflavonoids (see page 26), but it is preferable to get them from green tea.

As a substitute for coffee try Caro and Caro Extra, Bambu, and Yannoh which are grain "coffees" and contain various combinations of ingredients like barley, rye, chicory, and acorns.

Dandelion "coffee" can also be very useful. Don't buy the instant version as it contains lactose, but buy the roots. Dandelion helps to cleanse the liver – the organ of detoxification which also helps eliminate accumulated "old" female hormones – and reduce the risk of breast growths. Dandelion is also a natural diuretic, allowing excess fluid to be released without losing vital nutrients at the same time, which usually happens with other diuretics. Dandelion itself contains more vitamins and minerals than any other herb and is one of the best natural sources of potassium, which plays a vital role in the correct functioning of the heart.

What about decaffeinated coffee?

Although decaffeinated coffee does not contain caffeine, it still contains theobromine and theophylline, which are stimulants similar to caffeine. In addition, the decaffeinating process is a chemical one, not a natural one. If you experience breast discomfort, the cause could be methylxanthines, which are contained in decaffeinated coffee.

Alcohol

Alcohol, like tea and coffee, also acts as a diuretic. Therefore drinking wine with a meal could lose you some valuable nutrients. The message is again moderation. By all means have a glass of wine socially when you are out, but do not drink every evening with your dinner.

Alcohol is also full of calories: one glass of red or white wine gives 100 calories and a pint of beer around 200 calories. If you want to lose weight, reducing or eliminating your alcohol consumption for a while is a very effective method.

Too high an intake of alcohol will compromise the healthy functioning of the liver. As the liver converts the more carcinogenic estradiol into estriol and excretes it out of your body (see page 10), you want your liver to be working as efficiently as possible at menopause. If you damage your liver, "old" hormones could be circulating since your body cannot get rid of them.

Alcohol can also interfere with your metabolism of essential fatty acids. These are needed to produce prostaglandins, chemicals that help to control moods and vascular reactions like hot flashes.

As already made clear, unfortunately the benefits of wine to the heart are actually due to the skins of the grapes and not the alcohol.

What is best to drink?

Water would have to come top of the list – a simple, natural drink and yet easily forgotten. Your body is made up of approximately 70 percent water and it is involved in every function of the body. It helps transport nutrients and waste products in and out of the cells and it is also used to maintain body temperature – particularly vital at menopause.

Most of us do not drink enough water. Ironically, women who suffer from water retention tend to restrict their liquid intake thinking that the less they drink, the less their bodies will retain. Actually, the opposite is true. If you restrict fluids, your body tries to compensate by retaining more liquid just in case it is in short supply.

Some women, however, are drinking too much liquid. You can gauge this by the amount of times you need to pass urine. If you get up often during the night or find that you are going very frequently during the day, then experiment by cutting down. We need to drink around six glasses of water a day, which includes any herb teas you might drink. It does not include ordinary tea and coffee because of their diuretic effect. A wonderful way to start the day is a cup of hot water with a slice of lemon, which is very cleansing for the liver.

To ensure purified water at home, use either a jug filter (available from chemists, supermarkets and health food stores) or have a filter plumbed into your water system, fitted under the sink.

Bottled water

The different kinds of bottled water can be confusing, so here is a simple guide:

✱ Spring water – may have been taken from one or more underground sources and have undergone a range of treatments, such as filtration and blending.
✱ Natural mineral water – bottled in its natural underground state and not treated in any way. It has to come from an officially registered source, conform to purity standards and carry details of its source and mineral analysis on the label.
✱ Natural sparkling water – natural water from its underground source with enough natural carbon dioxide to make it bubbly. Again, untreated and utterly natural.
✱ Sparkling (carbonated) water – has had carbon dioxide added during bottling, just as with ordinary carbonated drinks.

The most natural waters, and therefore preferable to drink, are the natural mineral water and the natural sparkling water.

Additives, preservatives, and other chemicals

As well as buying organic food to reduce your intake of estrogen-mimicking pesticides, try to buy your food in its most natural state. You want to make it as easy as possible for your body to reach optimum health and stay there. Manufacturers often argue that additives, preservatives, and flavorings are used in such small quantities that they will not have any adverse effects. However, when you amass all the small amounts in all the different products you eat and drink every day, these small amounts soon add up. We are gradually creating a chemical cocktail inside ourselves, and nobody knows how exactly these chemicals will react together. Your body has to deal with these chemicals, with the result that energy and valuable nutrients are spent when they could be used for more profitable ends, such as disease prevention.

Genetically modified foods

Genes are a set of coded instructions made from DNA which control physical and behavioral characteristics such as hair color, etc.

Genetic engineering is about manipulating the basic DNA of a plant or animal. This happens naturally in evolution of course, but with nature in charge the process is normally slow and gradual taking hundreds of years. It is this process that ensures the fittest of the species survive. The gene manipulation that humans are now tinkering with bypasses evolution, and as yet we don't know what the price for this will be.

With genetic engineering, genes from other species are introduced into a particular plant to make them more resistant to pests, viruses, or weed-killers. For instance, it is now possible to buy a tomato which contains a fish gene to boost its frost resistance. The gene comes from the flounder because it survives well in cold water. This same flounder gene has also been introduced into salmon. In the cold dark days of winter a salmon stops eating and growing, but adding a flounder gene keeps them eating all year round, speeding up their growth rate by 400 percent.

When genes are transferred in the lab, marker genes are transferred along with the DNA. This enables scientists to identify which cells have become modified. Usually a gene for antibiotic resistance is used as a marker. The British Medical Association (BMA) fears that resistance to antibiotics might transfer to animals or humans, leaving patients vulnerable to diseases such as meningitis. For example, genetically modified maize contains a marker gene which passes on a resistance to ampicillin – an important antibiotic used to treat bronchitis, ear infections, and urinary tract infections in humans. In another instance, a nut gene was inserted into a soybean which was potentially fatal for people who are allergic to nuts. In this way it is all too easy for somebody with an allergy problem not to have any idea what they are eating. It is also possible for the DNA from GM foods to be transferred to the natural bacteria in the gut, creating lethal substances and a whole generation of new diseases which could not be killed off by antibiotics.

Some organizations are making a stand against these so-called "Frankenstein" foods. The BMA has issued a report called the "Impact of Genetic Modification on Agriculture, Food and Health" and has called for studies to see whether the foods could damage the immune system or cause birth defects.

My advice is to avoid genetically modified foods by reading the labels and buying organic where possible. If a food contains soy oil or lecithin, you should be suspicious because there are no obligations for it to be labelled "genetically modified." I used to buy my canned tuna in soy oil and have now switched to tuna in spring water. If we as consumers consciously do not buy these foods then eventually there may not be a market for them.

What about genetically modified soya?
This is an important subject because soy is the best-known genetically modified food and up to 60 percent of processed foods contain soy, including bread, biscuits, pizza, and baby food.

A high percentage of that soy will have been genetically modified. Lecithin, a substance contained in many foods, is also made from soy.

Greenpeace estimates that 90 percent of foods containing genetically modified products will be unlabeled, so you won't be able to make an informed choice about be able to make an informed choice about what you are buying. At the moment, if a food is organic, it is much less likely to be genetically modified.

The power of food

Phytonutrients, or plant compounds, are now the buzz word in science for all those plant compounds in food that can help to prevent disease and keep you healthy. At the moment more than 100 phytonutrients have been identified, including phytoe-strogens, bioflavonoids, beta-carotene and lycopene, indoles, and proantho-cyanidins. We cannot store these wonderful substances so we have to include them in our diet on a regular basis in order to reap their benefits.

Marvelously, nature has packed them into many of the foods we eat. The recipes that follow are full of phytonutrients to help alleviate the symptoms of menopause and to prevent those problems that can occur around that time, such as heart disease, osteoporosis and breast cancer.

So, I invite you to enjoy eating your way through menopause.

Bon Appétit!

from the chef

Let your food be your medicine and let your medicine be your food – Hippocrates

These recipes are specifically designed to benefit women approaching and at menopause by including certain health-giving ingredients. The introduction to and nutritional information about each recipe explains in what ways that particular dish is helpful.

Many of the breakfasts and snacks can provide you with your daily supply of phytoestrogens without having to involve the rest of your family in the diet. It is much more productive, however, to vary your meals so that you access the whole range of important ingredients. I would therefore suggest you use as broad a sweep as possible of the dishes, including appetizers, main courses, and desserts. Most women tend to avoid desserts for fear of putting on weight, but it is the sugar in recipes and the tendency to use a lot of dairy products that makes desserts unhealthy. As this book demonstrates, it is in fact possible to create sweet but healthy desserts without using sugar.

In Japan a typical daily menu for the whole family would be:

Breakfast: miso soup containing seaweed and tofu, rice, and often a side dish of fish

Lunch: vegetable and egg dish in miso soup with rice

Dinner: miso soup with rice, a tofu dish with sesame sauce, fish, boiled greens, and pickles

This shows quite how many phytoestrogens are conventionally eaten by the Japanese, regardless of gender or age. Japanese menopausal women may be lucky as this is their natural diet, but perhaps you are at more of an advantage, with access to a greater variety of dishes and styles – from French to Italian, Japanese to Thai, Indian to Mexican.

Such cuisine appeals to everyone, and if you can subtly introduce ingredients like soy and flax seeds into the whole family's diet, the cardiovascular and anti-cancer benefits will be available to them as well as you. For example, cows' milk is not an ideal food because of its high saturated fat content and its potential for generating mucus (and often catarrh), so adding soy milk in certain recipes instead of cows' milk can be a simple change but extremely beneficial.

How to manage when your routine is interrupted

Women often ask me what they should do when they are traveling, staying with friends or socializing and cannot control the foods that are being served to them. The answer is to do the best you can, within the limits.

If you are entertained by friends, enjoy the meal with the generosity with which it has been made. Eating, after all, is a social occasion. Even if you end up with a piece of chocolate cake for dessert, it is difficult to refuse and such an exception does not matter so long as your foundation at home is good.

If you have to buy a sandwich for a quick lunch at work, buy one with whole-wheat bread and with a healthy filling such as tuna. It is much easier when you are at a restaurant, as you can usually have fish with vegetables or a salad. However, only at Indian, Middle Eastern, or Japanese restaurants will you eat the most important phytoestrogens such as soy, lentils, and chickpeas. If you are away from home for more than a few days or if you are eating on the run frequently, then it would be a good idea to take a good multivitamin and mineral supplement designed for menopause such as the Natural Health Practice's Menoplus (see page 157, Shopper's Guide) which you can mail order.

shopping and cooking tips

To benefit truly from the recipes in this book, here are some guidelines.

Alcohol
Some of the recipes call for a drop or two of alcohol, especially the desserts. This is of course optional, and can be saved for special occasions – they are usually equally delicious without. Some grated orange zest can give much the same effect as an addition of Grand Marnier, for instance.

Aluminum
Aluminum is a toxic metal which interferes with the body's ability to metabolize calcium. It can accumulate in the bones, restricting the formation of new bone – which is essential to prevent osteoporosis. You should therefore avoid using aluminum saucepans, as the toxins can enter the food through cooking. The same applies to aluminum foil and aluminum containers. Instead, use cast iron, enamel, glass, and stainless-steel cookware. Avoid any coated or non-stick pans, as the coating can eventually wear off into the food.

Beans
Ideally, beans should be cooked from raw but for convenience you can now buy beans already cooked; make sure you buy them in salt rather than sugar. Some supermarkets and healthfood stores have cans of organic beans.

When cooking beans, add a one-inch piece of kombu (a Japanese form of kelp) to the pan. The seaweed helps to cook the beans more quickly and also to break down the substances that are responsible for causing flatulence! As seaweed has an extremely good mineral content, the valuable nutrients will transfer to the water in which the beans are cooked. You can either remove the kombu after cooking or, if you are going to blend the beans, you could leave the seaweed in and enjoy all the extra goodness. Never salt beans until halfway through cooking, otherwise the skins toughen.

Citrus fruit
If the recipe calls for the zest of an orange or lemon, try to buy uncoated fruit. Any citrus fruit that is not labeled "unwaxed" will be preserved with a chemical wax, which you do not want to add to your cooking. Uncoated fruit does not keep very long, so be sure to buy it shortly before using.

Custard
Natural custard powder is available from healthfood stores. It contains cornflour and natural coloring. You can make the custard with soy milk instead of cows' milk, and maple syrup instead of sugar. This custard is excellent for pouring over apple pies and crumbles made with whole-wheat flour. Otherwise, try it over a trifle made using the sugarless sponge recipe (see page 146), and fresh or canned fruit (in fruit juice, not syrup).

Dairy products
Keep the number of dishes containing dairy foods down to a minimum per day and always buy organic.

Butter
Some of the recipes do use butter, but sparingly. Remember that olive oil is always an option instead of butter for cooking purposes.

Cheese
Watch out for a rennet called chymosin which is used to harden cheese as it can sometimes be genetically modified. On some cheeses the label specifies that it is GM free. If you prefer, you can omit the cheese from a recipe where applicable.

Cream
The cream in any of the recipes – particularly the desserts – is optional and should ideally be kept for special occasions. Organic plain live yogurt or soy yogurt makes a healthier substitute, or you can puree silken tofu, as in the Strawberry Shortcake recipe (see page 135).

Yogurt
Buy live organic yogurt which contains a culture such as lactobacillus acidophilus, which is a natural inhabitant of your gut.

Dried fruits
When buying dried fruits, avoid any that contain the preserving agent sulphur dioxide. Sulphur dioxide occurs naturally but is produced chemically for commercial use. It is suspected of being a factor in genetic mutations and an irritant to the alimentary food canal. The preservative is used most often on dried apricots to keep their pretty orange color. Those that are free from preservatives will look brown but taste fine. Supermarket dried fruits such as mixed fruit, raisins, sultanas, etc., will often have mineral oil added to them. This gives them a shiny appearance and keeps them separate. You should try to steer clear of this kind of oil as it can interfere with your absorption of calcium and phosphorus. Furthermore, as mineral oil passes through your body, it can pick up and excrete the oil-soluble

vitamins (A, D, E and K), which your body wants to retain.

Eggs
Egg sizes in the recipes are medium, unless otherwise stated.

Garam masala
Garam masala paste tends to have sugar added to it, whereas powder doesn't. It is advisable to cook the powder gently in a tablespoon of oil for a few minutes before using.

Meat and poultry
We have to watch how much animal protein we eat at menopause because of the leeching effect on the bones, so neither red meat, game, nor poultry are used in the recipes. As mentioned on page 31, red meat also takes a long time to digest and therefore can increase the risk of bowel cancer. If you do choose to eat animal protein, the best for your general health is fish, with eggs the next in line.

Oils
Look for cold-pressed unrefined organic oils. It is important to store oils out of the light and away from heat to prevent oxidation, which invites attack by free radicals.

Flaxseed oil
This is recommended for salad dressings because of its phytoestrogen content. However, it is very delicate and should never be heated. It can go rancid very quickly and so needs to be kept in the fridge. It is therefore better to buy smaller quantities of linseed oil.

Olive oil
It is better to cook with olive oil because there is less danger of creating free radicals, which have been connected to aging and cancer. The recipes in this book use olive oil unless the oil does not need to be heated. To lessen the possibility of free radical damage further, only fry at low temperatures or, even better, first put a little water in the pan, heat that up and then add in the oil. This stops it from reaching too high a temperature. For salad dressings use extra virgin olive oil.

Sesame oil
The dark version is made from lightly toasted seeds and has a stronger flavor but less goodness. Sesame oil is for dressings only.

Soy oil
Unfortunately, soy oil does not contain any isoflavones but it does contain both Omega 3 and Omega 6 oils, which makes it ideal for salad dressings. It is important that you buy organic as it is less likely to be genetically modified.

Walnut oil
This has a powerful flavor and is good on dressings, but in moderation. Never heat it.

Organic
Buy organic wherever possible, be it bread, flour, fruit, vegetables, soy milk, or free-range eggs.

Sauces
If a recipe calls for tomato ketchup or mayonnaise and you are short of time, look for the excellent organic versions which are available in supermarkets and

healthfood stores. Ideally, use the recipes for them given in Basic Recipes (see pages 152–153).

Seasonings
Salt and pepper are listed in most recipes, but it is up to you how much you use. I tend to cook with minimal amounts of sea salt and no pepper. I just use salt to cook grains like rice and millet and otherwise use soy sauce and other flavorings such as garlic, ginger, and lemon for vegetable dishes. We only need about 4g of salt a day (a level teaspoon of salt weighs 5g), otherwise we retain fluid. As with all things, we don't want too little or too much; an excess of salt can contribute to high blood pressure. Do not add salt at the table but use it only in the cooking, and choose sea salt or low-salt alternatives such as Lo-Salt. They do not contain the chemicals that are added to table salt in order to make it flow freely

Seaweeds
There are a number of different varieties of seaweed. Nori is used by the Japanese to make a form of sushi (wrapped around rice with cucumber or fish in the middle). It is usually bought in sheets and toasted in the oven or over a low flame, where it changes from brown to green; otherwise buy the pretoasted variety. It can be crumbled and used as a condiment added to rice, pasta or soups. Kombu, the Japanese equivalent of kelp, is very helpful in preventing the flatulence which can be induced by beans; its use is described under "Beans" (see page 40).

Agar is an easy introduction to seaweeds and is used in some of the dessert recipes. It doesn't look like a seaweed as it comes in the form of white flakes. It can be used to set any liquid, so is excellent to make fruit jellies instead of using gelatin (which is ground-up bones). The rule of thumb is to use one tablespoon of agar flakes to set one cup of liquid or, if you are using agar powder, one teaspoon of powder will set ½ pint (1¼ cups) of liquid. Sprinkle the flakes or powder over the liquid and bring to a simmer without stirring. Simmer for approximately three minutes, stirring occasionally, until the flakes or powder have dissolved. Then transfer to a dish or mold and leave to set at room temperature.

Seeds

Feel free to sprinkle on extra seeds to vegetables or salads. In order to include beneficial quantities of essential fatty acids as well as phytoestrogens, an effective mix would be one part each of sesame, sunflower, and pumpkin mixed with two parts flax seeds. Store the mix in a sealed container in the fridge, and lightly grind the quantity you need just before serving. Tahini paste is made from crushed sesame seeds.

When seeds are cooked at high temperatures, it destroys their valuable nutrients and creates free radicals, which is why it is better to eat them raw or very lightly toasted. However, if they are cooked inside breads or cakes, the temperature is low enough to preserve the oil's qualities. When eating flax seeds, make sure you drink lots of fluids.

Soy products

When buying soy products like tofu and soy milk, try to buy organic. Some companies like the European Provamel have guaranteed that their products do not contain any genetically modified ingredients.

Miso

This is a dark brown soybean paste. It is made from whole soybeans combined with barley or rice, with a mold culture added. The mixture is left to ferment for one to three years. The paste is excellent as a kind of broth, added to soups or stews. Because of the fermentation process, miso contains enzymes which are beneficial for digestion. Once miso is added to soup, the soup should not be boiled again but kept simmering – otherwise the beneficial enzymes could be destroyed. It is best to put miso into a separate bowl with a little hot water or broth and stir to make it into a smooth, slightly runny paste before adding it to the stew or soup.

It is also possible to buy instant miso (soybean paste) soups. The company Westbrae make two varieties – one with tofu and the other with seaweed – which are available in healthfood stores. As it is so simple to make (it only needs hot water), I often have a mug of it to start the day when I arrive at the clinic, instead of herbal tea.

Soy milk

Made from whole soybeans, soy milk can be used on its own on cereals and in place of cows' milk in any recipe. Soy milk contains more protein than milk without the saturated fat or cholesterol. The various brands of soya milk will taste different, so do not give up if you do not like the taste of the first one you buy. Some are sweetened with apple juice, and you could experiment by adding spices like cinnamon and nutmeg. I use soy milk to make a milky coffee by heating the milk and adding it to an instant coffee such as Folgers. For an extra treat I add a drizzle of pure maple syrup.

Soy sauce

This serves an excellent purpose as a flavoring, but as you only need a dash at a time it is not possible to obtain many phytoestrogens from it. Make sure you buy one which is free from added monosodium glutamate. The wheat-free version is called tamari.

Tempeh

This is another form of soy with such an acquired taste that it is not used in any of the recipes in the book, but you may like to try it. It is made from fermenting soybeans pressed into a block. Tempeh has a strong taste and can be fried or used in soups.

Tofu

This is soybean curd and is made by adding a curdling agent to soy milk. It is a solid white block and can either be bought as firm tofu or silken, which is soft. The firm tofu is easier to cut into cubes and so is ideal for stir-fries. The silken is best used when you want to blend ingredients such as in a dessert, because it is so soft. Tofu has no taste of its own so its flavor is dependent on what you cook with it.

Because of this ability to pick up the flavor of the food it is combined with and because it can be prepared in a variety of ways, it is wonderfully versatile. It can be sliced, cubed, mashed, scrambled, pureed and used in both savory and sweet dishes. You can buy tofu in supermarkets; many will have organic tofu. If you do not use a whole pack of tofu at once, put the remaining portion in a bowl, cover with water, and leave in the fridge.

Sugar

Many products have "hidden" sugar in them. Avoid ingredients that contain sugar as there are usually excellent alternatives. For instance, Worcestershire sauce normally contains sugar but a company called Life and Health has one with no added sugar or salt. As several of the recipes here include Worcestershire sauce, it is certainly worth getting hold of this version; after all, it will last a long time.

If you crave something sweet, it is possible to make a sweet dessert, pastry, cookie, or cake without adding sugar. Maple syrup, date syrup, rice syrup, barley malt, and honey are excellent sweeteners and much better for you. Remember that the key is moderation. Putting lashings of honey on your toast every day is not a good idea, but using it in a cake recipe or drizzling it over porridge is fine. Do not substitute artificial sweeteners or fructose for sugar.

Whole-wheat

Use whole-wheat/wholegrain products for foods such as flour, pasta, rice, and bread. Plain white flour contains the bleaching agent sulphur dioxide, which is produced chemically and may cause genetic mutations. Doppio zero flour is an Italian product used to make fresh pasta, and is increasingly available in supermarkets and delicatessens.

Quantity of phytoestrogens

You should be aiming to eat one serving of soy a day, which is equal to approximately two ounces tofu, one pint soy milk or two ounces soy flour. This will give you approximately 35 to 40mg of isoflavones. Your daily intake should also ideally include one tablespoon of linseeds.

As with anything, too much of one thing can be just as bad as too little. For example, if you ate too many carrots you could literally turn orange! So don't just use soy but remember that other legumes also contain good amounts of phytoestrogens. These include chickpeas and lentils – so a portion of hummus added to a salad is excellent for you, especially since the sesame in the hummus also gives you a high quantity of calcium.

Nutritional value of each recipe

There is a system of asterisks to illustrate the nutritional content of the recipes. P stands for phytoestrogens, E for essential fatty acids, and A is antioxidants. An award of five stars (*****) represents the highest value and one (*) the lowest. The phytoestrogen content is only an estimate because plant estrogens can vary according to brand, e.g., no two makes of soy milk contain the exact same amount of phytoestrogens. Although research has been extensive into soy products, not all foods have yet been analyzed scientifically for their phytoestrogen content – e.g., rice. Levels of fiber have not been evaluated because it will occur naturally and in good quantities in these dishes.

1

breakfasts and brunches

strawberry smoothie

This is a refreshing summer drink to set you up for the day. It delivers good amounts of phytoestrogens and antioxidants. Strawberries contain more vitamin C than any other berry so they are good for the immune system and also help to produce collagen for skin and bone health.

8 ounces strawberries, sliced (about 1 cup)
1 cup soy milk
1 tablespoon frozen orange juice concentrate, thawed
1 banana, chopped
Honey to taste (optional)

Makes about 2–3 good glasses

Put all the ingredients in a food processor with a handful of ice cubes and process until smooth. If necessary, sweeten to taste with a little honey.

P *** E ** A ****
SOY MILK IS A GOOD SOURCE OF PHYTOESTROGENS AND THE FRUIT PROVIDES ANTIOXIDANTS.

perfect porridge

Oats, which make an excellent warming breakfast, are one of the best foods for keeping cholesterol under control. The dried fruit contains potassium, which helps with water retention. A berry puree will give you extra antioxidants by way of their bioflavonoids, which strengthen the collagen in the bone matrix, so helping to prevent osteoporosis.

⅔ cup oatmeal
1¾ cups soy milk
⅓ cup soy cream
3 tablespoons orange juice
1 teaspoon ground cinnamon
3 tablespoons maple syrup
⅓ cup seedless raisins
⅓ cup dried figs, chopped
⅓ cup dried apricots, chopped

⅓ cup seedless raisins
⅓ cup dried figs, chopped
⅓ cup dried apricots, chopped
Additional maple syrup, or a fresh fruit puree or Dried Fruit Compote (see page 48), for serving

Serves 4

If using coarse oatmeal, first soak it in water overnight.

Put the oatmeal (well drained if necessary) in a large heavy-bottomed saucepan and add the soy milk. Bring to a boil, lower the heat and then simmer for 20–30 minutes for coarse oatmeal, or three to four minutes (check the package's instructions) for porridge or rolled oats.

Remove the pan from the heat and allow to cool slightly.

When cooler, stir in the soy cream, orange juice, cinnamon and maple syrup and mix well. Then stir in the dried fruit.

You can either serve the porridge warm or cold, topped with some more maple syrup or a fresh fruit puree, such as raspberry or strawberry, or Dried Fruit Compote (see page 48).

P ***** E ** A ****
OATS, SOY MILK, SOY CREAM, AND CINNAMON ARE ALL SOURCES OF PHYTOESTROGENS.

homemade luxury muesli

It is wonderful to think that you can gain so many nutrients in just one breakfast. Oats and barley are excellent sources of fiber, noted for their ability to reduce heart disease. The fruit provides you with good amounts of vitamin C, and the live organic yogurt is recommended for the digestive system as it contains beneficial bacteria.

4 tablespoons rolled oats
4 tablespoons barley kernels
    or flakes
½ cup soy flour
4 tablespoons raisins
⅓ cup dried apricots,
    chopped into chunks
2 large oranges
2 dessert apples
2 pears
Juice of 1 lemon
4 tablespoons good quality runny
    honey or maple syrup
4 tablespoons unsalted mixed
    nuts, chopped
1 tablespoon flax seeds
1 tablespoon sunflower seeds
1 tablespoon sesame seeds
Soy milk and organic live plain
    yogurt, for serving

Serves 4

The night before, put the oats, barley, soy flour, and dried fruit in a bowl. Shred the peel from one of the oranges and squeeze the juice of both. Add these to the bowl (along with any orange pulp that gathers in the grater) and toss well to mix. Leave to soak overnight.

In the morning, coarsely grate the unpeeled apples and pears on top of the soaked grains. Pour over the lemon juice. Add the honey or maple syrup and the chopped nuts, and mix well.

Finish by sprinkling with the flax seeds, sunflower, and sesame seeds. Serve with soy milk and some plain yogurt.

P **** E ***** A *****
PHYTOESTROGENS IN THE SOY FLOUR, SEEDS, OATS, AND BARLEY. THE NUTS AND SEEDS SUPPLY EFAS; APRICOTS ARE RICH IN THE ANTIOXIDANT BETA-CAROTENE.

french toast

You can use all types of bread for French toast, or *pain perdu* (lost bread), as long as it is old enough to be dryish, or it will absorb too much of the egg and fall apart on cooking. Try it with whole-wheat bread, brioche, or challah, sliced baguette, or even croissants. This dish should really be kept as a treat, although it has a good helping of phytoestrogens.

4 eggs
Pinch of freshly ground sea salt
1 cup soy milk
½ teaspoon vanilla extract
½ teaspoon ground cinnamon,
    plus more to serve
Butter or olive oil, for greasing
8 slices slightly stale bread (see
    above)
Maple syrup, Dried Fruit
Compote (see page 48), or fresh
    berries, for serving

Serves 8

In a bowl, beat the eggs lightly and add the salt, soy milk, vanilla, and cinnamon. Beat again until frothy.

Grease a griddle pan lightly with butter or oil and get it hot. Dip each slice of bread into the egg mixture until it is well coated and cook on the hot griddle pan until well browned on both sides (you may have to do this in batches and keep warm).

Serve sprinkled with more cinnamon and some maple syrup, Dried Fruit Compote (see page 48) or soft fruit like raspberries and blueberries.

Variation: try adding the grated peel and juice of one large orange to the egg mixture.

P ** E * A *
THE SOY MILK AND WHOLE-WHEAT BREAD ARE BOTH SOURCES OF PHYTOESTROGENS.

dried fruit compote with gingered yogurt

If you ever have a sugar craving, dried fruit is sweet as well as healthy, and is also useful in alleviating constipation. Dried figs are high in the soluble fiber pectin, which helps lower cholesterol levels. Both figs and apricots are rich in potassium, which helps with water retention.

3 ounces dried apple rings, cut in half
3 ounces dried figs, cut into bite-sized pieces
3 ounces dried apricots, cut into bite-sized pieces
1½ ounces dried banana slices
1½ ounces dried pineapple slices, broken up into pieces
1½ ounces golden raisins

⅔ cup dry cider
⅔ cup orange or apple juice
¼ cinnamon stick
1 tablespoon orange flower water, to serve
For the gingered yogurt
Large chunk of fresh ginger root
2 tablespoons maple or date syrup, warmed
1½ cups runny plain yogurt, preferably soy yogurt

Serves 4–6

Put the dried fruit in a saucepan and pour over the cider and fruit juice. Drop in the cinnamon stick. Bring gently to just below boiling point, cover and simmer very gently for 15 minutes. Take off the heat and leave the fruit to soak and cool for at least one hour, ideally overnight.

To make the gingered yogurt: press the ginger through a garlic press and stir the resulting juice into the syrup. Stir that into the yogurt.

Remove the cinnamon stick from the compote (you can leave it in for presentation if you like, but do make sure no one crunches into it). Serve hot, warm, or cold, sprinkled with the orange flower water and accompanied by the yogurt.

P * E * A ****
DRIED FRUIT CONTAINS HIGH AMOUNTS OF ANTIOXIDANTS, AND THESE ARE FURTHERED BY THE ORANGE OR APPLE JUICE.

middle-eastern pancakes

The culture in live organic yogurt is excellent for intestinal health. Almonds supply essential fatty acids, the oils that we need to lubricate our joints and skin, and are an excellent source of vitamin E, an antioxidant. Dates are high in magnesium as well as potassium, so useful in reducing water retention.

For the batter
¾ cup all-purpose flour, preferably whole-wheat
¼ cup soy flour
Pinch of freshly ground sea salt
⅔ cup plain yogurt
1 egg
⅔–¾ cup soy milk
Finely grated peel of ½ lemon

For the filling
¾ cup ground almonds
White of 1 egg, lightly beaten
1 tablespoon orange flower water
3 tablespoons date syrup
Finely grated peel of ½ lemon
2 teaspoons ground cinnamon
1 cup pitted dates, chopped
Butter or oil, for greasing and frying

For the topping
Juice of 1 lemon
2 tablespoons date syrup
½ cup pistachios, chopped

Serves 4–6 (makes about 12)

First make the pancake batter: sift the flours and salt into a large bowl. Make a well in the center, add the yogurt, break in the egg, and beat until smooth. Gradually beat in the soy milk and then add the lemon peel. Allow to stand, covered, for about 20 minutes.

Make the filling: in a bowl, mix together the ground almonds, egg white, orange flower water, and date syrup until smooth. Stir in the lemon peel, cinnamon, and the dates.

Preheat a hot broiler.

Lightly grease a seven-inch pancake pan with butter or oil and place over a high heat. When it is hot, reduce the heat to moderate and pour a tablespoon of batter into the pan. Tilt the pan to spread it all over the base of the pan. Cook for one minute, then flip the pancake over and fry the other side for the same time. Turn out on a sheet of parchment paper and fold that over to keep it warm. Repeat with the rest of the batter, wiping and greasing the pan between each pancake. Pile the pancakes on top of one another, with a layer of parchment paper between each.

Put a heaped spoonful of the filling in the center of each pancake and fold it over, then fold in the ends and roll it up. Grease a heatproof dish just big enough to take the pancakes in a single layer and arrange them in it.

For the topping: stir the lemon juice in to the date syrup and spoon over the pancakes. Sprinkle with the pistachios and broil until the syrup is bubbling and the pancakes have darkened in color slightly.

Serve with dollops of more yogurt and a little date syrup.

P *** E *** A *
PHYTOESTROGENS ARE PRESENT IN THE SOY FLOUR, SOY MILK, WHOLE-WHEAT FLOUR AND CINNAMON. EFAS FROM THE PISTACHIOS.

breakfast muffins

Muffins for breakfast may seem naughty, but this recipe is full of goodness. The proanthocyanidins in the blueberries and cranberries play a major part in the prevention of heart disease and strokes. As they help to preserve the integrity of the capillaries they play a role in preventing varicose veins. These excellent antioxidants also contribute towards osteoporosis prevention because of their effect on collagen: by cross-linking collagen fibers, they strengthen the collagen matrix and stop its destruction. Nuts and dried fruits are particularly rich in nutrients and the B vitamins in the pecan nuts are often classed as "calming foods." Apricots contain high levels of potassium, beneficial for reducing high blood pressure and water retention, and their beta-carotene levels are increased in their drying.

Olive oil for greasing
1¾ cups all-purpose flour, preferably whole-wheat
3 tablespoons soy flour
Pinch of freshly ground sea salt
2 teaspoons baking powder
2 eggs
½ stick butter, melted
⅔–¾ cup soy milk
½ cup maple syrup
½ cup fresh blueberries
½ cup dried cranberries, chopped
½ cup seedless raisins
¼ cup dried apricots, chopped
½ cup pecans, chopped
1 teaspoon grated orange peel
1 teaspoon ground cinnamon

Makes 12

Preheat the oven to 400°F and, using olive oil, grease some muffin pans with two-and-a-half-inch diameter indentations. Sift the flours, salt, and baking powder into a bowl. In another bowl, lightly beat the eggs, then stir in the melted butter, soy milk, and maple syrup. Pour this into the bowl of flour, then add the remaining ingredients, and combine quickly without overworking (it's fine if there are a few lumps left in the mixture – you want it sticky rather than fluid). Spoon the mixture into the muffin pans.

Bake for 20–25 minutes until well risen and browned. Leave to cool in the pans for a few minutes before turning out, then allow to cool completely before serving, or storing in an airtight container.

These muffins are great on their own, and even tastier accompanied by butter with honey or sugar-free jelly. They also make a good portable high-phyto snack for getting you through the day.

Variation: if you like and you have the time, you can first plump up the dried fruit by soaking it in the juice from the orange, tossing from time to time, for about 30 minutes. This gives an even more moist result.

P ***** E ** A *****
PHYTOESTROGENS IN THE SOY FLOUR, SOY MILK, WHOLE-WHEAT FLOUR, CINNAMON, CRANBERRIES, AND ORANGE PEEL. EFAS FROM THE PECAN NUTS.

kedgeree

The spices benefit the digestive system: cumin is traditionally known to help counter flatulence, cardamom is used to aid digestion, and cayenne acts as a general tonic for the digestive system. For brunch, you can give more of a savory punch by frying one or two sliced onions with a couple of garlic cloves until crisp. Mix these in or sprinkle them over the top.

1¼ cups brown basmati rice
1⅓ cups split red lentils
About 1 pound undyed
   smoked haddock
About ⅔ cup soy milk
1–2 bay leaves
1 cinnamon stick
4–5 black peppercorns
6 cardamom pods
1 lime, plus more to serve
   (optional)

Large handful of flat-leaf parsley,
   plus more for garnishing
Large handful of cilantro, plus
   more for garnishing
3–4 tablespoons soy cream
Pinch of ground cumin
Freshly ground sea salt and black
   pepper
Pinch or two of cayenne pepper
2–3 hard-boiled eggs, cut
   into wedges

Serves 4–6

First put the rice and lentils to soak in a large bowl, covered generously with water.

Rinse the haddock well under cold running water and put it in a saucepan with soy milk barely to cover (cut the fish into manageable pieces if necessary). Add a bay leaf or two, half the cinnamon stick, and the black peppercorns, and bring to a boil. Poach gently for two to four minutes, until the fish is stiff and beginning to flake (the exact time will depend on how thick it is). Drain and let the fish cool a little.

When the fish is cool enough to handle, flake it into a bowl, taking some care to remove any remaining bones. Put a large pot of lightly salted water on to boil. Lightly crush the cardamom pods and add to the water with the rest of the cinnamon. Drain the soaking rice and lentils into a strainer and rinse thoroughly under cold running water until the water runs clear.

Tip the rice and lentils into the heating water and bring to a boil. Stir, cover and cook until both the rice and lentils are just tender, 20–30 minutes depending on variety and age.

When the rice and lentils are ready, drain thoroughly. Return to the saucepan and fish out the pieces of cinnamon and cardamom. Place over a very low heat and fork the rice once or twice to help it dry off. Grate in the peel of the lime and pour in the juice. Snip in most of the parsley and cilantro. Add the soy cream with the cumin stirred into it. Stir well over medium heat to warm everything through and then add the fish. Season to taste with salt, pepper, and cayenne.

Turn out into a warmed serving dish, dot all over with the wedges of hard-boiled egg and garnish with the reserved flat-leaf parsley and a few cilantro leaves. Serve with lime wedges, if you like.

P ***** E ** A ****
AN EXCELLENT VARIETY OF PHYTOESTROGENS FROM THE SOY MILK, SOY CREAM, LENTILS, BROWN RICE, CINNAMON, AND PARSLEY.

papaya with smoked fish mousse

With its bright colors, this is a very pretty dish as well as having a wonderful flavor. Mackerel is very good for the health because of its high levels of essential fatty acids in the form of Omega 3 oils. The soy cream provides phytoestrogens in good supply.

2 papayas
1 lime
For the mousse
12 ounces smoked mackerel fillets, skinned
⅔ cup soy cream
Juice of 1 lime, plus more if necessary
Freshly ground sea salt and black pepper
1–2 tablespoon(s) horseradish cream
Tabasco sauce

Serves 4–6

First make the mousse: flake the fish into a large bowl and add the soy cream and lime juice. Using a fork, mix well to a smoothish puree. Season with salt and pepper, horseradish, Tabasco, and more lime juice to taste.

Halve the papayas, scoop out the seeds, and then peel off the skins. You can then either serve the mousse spooned into the cavities (take a little sliver off the base of each papaya half so they will sit stably) or slice each half almost all the way across lengthwise, fan it out, and set the mousse alongside. Either way, squeeze lime juice over all the papaya flesh to prevent discoloration, and sprinkle with some pepper.

P *** E *** A *
MACKEREL IS A GOOD SOURCE OF EFAS IN THE FORM OF OMEGA 3 OILS AND PHYTOESTROGENS ARE AVAILABLE IN THE SOY CREAM.

scrambled tofu

This is a wonderful way to start the day, and a much healthier alternative to the egg version. The soft tofu and parsley in the dish are packed full of phytoestrogens. Serve with whole-wheat bread or toast, or the Four-seed Loaf on page 138 together with with broiled tomatoes and mushrooms.

1 tablespoon fresh basil, shredded, or 1 teaspoon dried basil
2 tablespoons flat-leaf parsley, finely chopped
1 tablespoon soy sauce
2 teaspoons olive oil
2 scallions, chopped
8 ounces soft tofu, crumbled

Serves 4

In a bowl or using a pestle and mortar, mash together the basil, parsley, and soy sauce. Set aside.

Heat the oil in a skillet and, when hot, sauté the scallions until just wilted. Stir in the tofu followed by the herb mixture and stir-fry for another three to four minutes.

P **** E * A *
HIGH AMOUNTS OF PHYTOESTROGENS FROM THE TOFU AND PARSLEY. IF YOU SERVE WITH BROILED TOMATOES YOU WILL GAIN EXTRA ANTIOXIDANTS.

eggs florentine

Eggs are good for the health in many ways. Although they have a bad name because of their high cholesterol content, they are low in saturated fat and a healthy source of protein. The egg yolk contains lecithin, which helps lower the risk of heart disease by preventing plaque from accumulating in the arteries.

12 ounces spinach, stalks removed (about 9 cups)
Freshly ground sea salt and black pepper
½ ounce soy flour
2–3 tablespoons soy cream
Freshly grated nutmeg
4 slices whole-wheat bread
Butter or olive oil, for greasing and frying
A few drops of cider or red wine vinegar
4 very fresh eggs

For the Mornay sauce
1 tablespoon butter
2 tablespoons flour
1¼ cups soy milk
Freshly ground sea salt and black pepper
Freshly grated nutmeg
2 cups mature Cheddar cheese, grated

Serves 4

Put the spinach in a saucepan with only the water from washing it clinging to its leaves. Cover tightly and cook over a gentle heat for two minutes. Add a pinch of sea salt, cover again, increase the heat to medium and cook for about five minutes more until the spinach is tender.

Drain very thoroughly, squeezing out any excess moisture with the back of a spoon, and return to the pan.

Mix the soy flour into the soy cream with nutmeg to taste, and then combine this with the spinach. Simmer gently until thickened and no moisture runs from it when spooned to one side of the pan. Keep warm.

Preheat a hot broiler and bring a saucepan of water to a simmer for the eggs.

Cut out rounds from the slices of bread big enough to line the bases of four large ramekins or custard cups. Fry these in butter or olive oil until good and crisp on both sides.

While the croûtes are frying, make the Mornay sauce: melt the butter or oil in a heavy-bottomed saucepan and stir in the soy flour. Cook over medium heat for a minute or two until the flour mixture just begins to color. Then stir in the soy milk and whisk until smooth. Bring to a boil and simmer for about five minutes. Season to taste with salt, pepper, and nutmeg, and then stir in the cheese. Check the flavoring and adjust the seasoning if necessary. Keep warm.

Add a few drops of vinegar to the simmering water and poach the eggs gently until opaque, a few minutes. Pour some cold water into the pan to stop the eggs from cooking, but leave them in the water to keep warm.

Using butter or olive oil, grease the sides of the ramekins, put the croûtes in the bottom, and spoon the spinach mixture on top of that. Draining them well on a slotted spoon, set a poached egg on top of each, then pour over the Mornay sauce. Cook briefly under the hot broiler, until bubbling. Serve at once.

P **** E * A *
PHYTOESTROGENS ARE CONTAINED IN GOOD AMOUNTS IN THE SOY FLOUR AND SOY CREAM AS WELL AS THE WHOLE-WHEAT BREAD.

frittata foo yung

The shrimp are low in saturated fat and high in protein. They are also an excellent source of vitamin B12 and a good source of the mineral selenium, which acts as a powerful antioxidant in the fight against cancer and helps prevent premature aging. Celery has anti-inflammatory properties and its potassium helps to alleviate water retention.

6 eggs
Freshly ground sea salt and black pepper
3 tablespoons soy cream
2 teaspoons soy sauce, plus more for dressing
2 tablespoons olive oil
2–3 thin slices of ginger root, finely chopped
1 celery heart stalk, thinly sliced
6 scallions, chopped
7 ounces beansprouts
1 tablespoon flax seeds
3 ounces cooked peeled small shrimp (about 2/3 cup)
A few chive stalks, for garnishing (optional)

Serves 4

Preheat a hot broiler. Break the eggs into a large bowl and beat well until quite frothy. Season lightly with salt and well with pepper and stir in the soy cream. Add the soy sauce and mix well.

Heat half the oil in a wok or large skillet and, when hot, stir-fry the ginger, celery, and scallions until just wilted. Then add in the beansprouts, flax seeds, and shrimp, toss to coat, and heat through well – but make sure you do not overcook. Set aside and keep warm.

Brush the bottom and sides of a medium-sized heatproof skillet with the remaining oil and place over medium to high heat. As soon as the oil gets hot, stir the egg mixture well again and pour it into the pan.

Pull the edges of the solidifying egg into the center two or three times and then immediately add the stir-fried mixture on top of the eggs. Arrange uniformly over the top with a fork, pressing the filling ingredients into the egg, and continue to cook over a slightly reduced heat for about three minutes until it is firmly set on the base.

Put under the broiler as close to the heat as you can get. Grill until the top is just browned and set. Serve cut into wedges, garnished with a few whole chive stalks, and sprinkled with some more soy sauce if you like.

P *** E ** A ***
EXCELLENT PHYTOESTROGEN CONTENT: ISOFLAVONES FROM THE SOY CREAM AND COUMESTANS FROM THE BEAN SPROUTS.

2

soups,
appetizers,
and snacks

no-cook fresh tomato soup

This soup can make a feast of fairly ordinary tomatoes, if they are good and ripe. Tomatoes are an excellent source of the antioxidant lycopene, which is known to help protect cells from damage. For a creamier soup, just stir in ⅔ cup soy cream or ⅓–½ cup thick unset plain yogurt, ideally soy yogurt.

2¼ pounds very ripe tomatoes, skinned, stalk ends removed, and roughly chopped
Small handful of flat-leaf parsley
A few sprigs of basil, plus more for garnishing (optional)
2 tablespoons tomato paste
Freshly ground sea salt and black pepper
Dash of no-added-sugar Worcestershire sauce
½ teaspoon celery salt
2 teaspoons honey

Serves 4

To skin tomatoes fast, put them in a heatproof bowl and pour over boiling water. Leave for a minute and then pour off the water. The skins should then come off quite readily.

Put the tomatoes, herbs, and tomato paste in a food processor or blender and puree. Taste and adjust the seasoning with salt, pepper, Worcestershire sauce, celery salt, and honey.

Chill well (not for more than three hours or the fresh tomato taste will lessen) and stir well before serving. Sprinkle with some shredded basil leaves to serve.

P *** E ** A ****
PHYTOESTROGENS IN THE SOY CREAM OR YOGURT; SMALL AMOUNTS IN THE PARSLEY AND CELERY SALT. TOMATOES PROVIDE ANTIOXIDANTS.

no-cook fresh pea soup

Celery is anti-inflammatory, so is useful for joint pains and arthritis. It also contains potassium which helps prevent water retention. Scallions are good for the bones. The seaweed flakes contain trace minerals, especially iodine, which regulates the metabolism, which can seem "sluggish" at the menopause.

1½ pounds fresh shelled garden peas (about 4½ pounds in the pod)
4 scallions, quartered
2 celery heart stalks, roughly chopped
4½ cups boiling water, miso broth (see page 150), or vegetable broth (see page 151)
1–2 tablespoons arrowroot (optional)
Freshly ground sea salt and black pepper
Dash of no-added-sugar Worcestershire sauce
3½ ounces tofu cream (see page 183), ⅓–½ cup thick unset plain yogurt, preferably soy yogurt, or
⅔ cup heavy cream
1½ tablespoons mixed seaweed flakes
Small bunch of chives

Serves 4

Put the peas, scallions, and celery in a food processor or blender and puree. Pour and spoon out into a large bowl or pot and mix in the water or broth. Depending on the texture of the peas and your taste, you may want to thicken the mixture with some arrowroot. Taste and adjust the seasoning with salt, pepper, and a dash of Worcestershire sauce.

If serving cold, chill for as long as you can before serving. To serve, swirl some tofu cream, yogurt, or cream into each bowl and scatter with some seaweed and snipped chives.

If serving warm, add the tofu cream, yogurt, or cream and heat through gently, stirring. Again, sprinkle over the seaweed and snipped chives just before serving. The real traditionalist can add a teaspoon or two of chopped fresh mint and garnish with mint instead of chives. Save the heavy cream for special occasions.

P **** E ** A **
A VARIETY OF PHYTOESTROGENS FROM THE MISO, TOFU CREAM OR SOY YOGURT, PEAS, AND THE CELERY.

no-cook borscht

This traditional Eastern European soup makes great use of the highly nutritious vegetable, beet. Cooked beet has good levels of vitamin C and potassium, which help to control water retention. Cabbages belong to the family of highly-beneficial cruciferous vegetables which includes broccoli, Brussels sprouts and cauliflower.

12 ounces large beets, cooked, peeled, and cut into chunks
8 ounces red or Savoy cabbage, roughly chopped
4 scallions, quartered
1 garlic clove
2 celery heart stalks, roughly chopped
4 cups boiling water, miso broth (see page 150) or
    vegetable stock (see page 151)
⅔ cup sour cream, plus a little more for serving
1 tablespoon cider vinegar
Freshly ground sea salt and black pepper
Freshly grated nutmeg
Grated English cucumber (peel included), for serving
Grated horseradish, for serving (optional)

Serves 6–8

Put the beets, cabbage, scallions, garlic, and celery in a food processor or blender and puree. Pour and spoon out into a large bowl or pot and mix in the water, broth, sour cream and cider vinegar. Taste, and adjust the seasoning with salt, pepper, and nutmeg.

Chill thoroughly before serving. Swirl some more sour cream over the soup in each bowl and sprinkle with some grated cucumber. Grated horseradish is a nice finishing touch for those who like it hot.

P *** E ** A ****
PHYTOESTROGENS FROM THE MISO BROTH, GARLIC, AND CELERY. HIGH IN ANTIOXIDANTS, BEETS CONTAIN MORE NUTRIENTS COOKED THAN RAW.

gazpacho

This lovely summer dish is all the better for being made the day before and chilled overnight, to allow the flavors to develop over time. If possible, it should be served ice-cold. The soup is sometimes served with ice cubes floating in it, but that often dilutes it unacceptably. Instead, particularly if you want to add a sophisticated touch, for a dinner party, say, freeze some of your best extra virgin olive oil in an ice cube tray – dropping a few whole chervil or flat parsley leaves in each section – and float some of the resulting cubes in the soup. For an extra boost of phytoestrogens you can use an equal parts mixture of olive oil with linseed or walnut oil in the soup. The scallions offer bone protection and the oil is excellent for the heart and preventing degenerative illness.

1 pound vine-ripened or
   plum tomatoes, skinned
   (see page 58)
½ English cucumber
1 green pepper
1 yellow pepper
4 scallions
2 garlic cloves
Handful of mixed herbs, ideally
   including flat-leaf parsley, chives,
   chervil, and basil
2 tablespoons extra virgin
   olive oil
1–2 tablespoon(s) cider vinegar

1¼ cups canned tomato
   juice, chilled
Freshly ground sea salt
½ teaspoon paprika, or to
   taste
2 hard-boiled eggs, shelled
   and fairly finely chopped, for
   garnishing

For the garlic croutons
2 tablespoons extra virgin
   olive oil
1 garlic clove, finely chopped
3 slices whole-wheat bread,
   crusts removed and cubed

Serves 4

Remove the stalk ends from the tomatoes and coarsely chop the tomatoes.

Cut off a quarter of the piece of cucumber and set that aside. Peel the rest and chop it coarsely. Seed and coarsely chop the peppers. Trim and coarsely chop the scallions. Then take the unpeeled cucumber and chop it very finely. Do the same with one-quarter of each of the prepared vegetables. Put each into separate small bowls to hand round with the soup and set aside.

Put the coarsely chopped vegetables in a blender with the garlic cloves, the herbs, oil, vinegar, and a little of the tomato juice. Blend to a puree. Mix in the rest of the tomato juice and adjust the seasoning with salt and paprika (remember that chilling mutes flavors, so season well). Put the soup to chill in the refrigerator for at least an hour, preferably overnight.

While the soup is cooling, make the garlic croutons: in a skillet, heat the oil and fry the garlic until aromatic. Add the bread cubes and sauté, tossing to coat them with the oil and garlic and browning them uniformly. Turn out on paper towels to drain.

Serve the chilled soup with the bowls of diced vegetables, chopped egg, and croutons.

P * E ** A ****
ANTIOXIDANTS FROM THE TOMATOES, PEPPERS, AND CUCUMBERS.

ribollita

A lovely bean soup from Tuscany which makes a good warming lunch on a cold day. The carrots contain high levels of the antioxidant beta-carotene, useful in preventing cell damage; the lycopene in the tomatoes has the same function. The cabbage is excellent in cancer protection and the garlic is particularly good for the immune system.

1½ cups dried cannellini beans
4 tablespoons olive oil
2 onions, finely chopped
2 leeks, finely chopped
2 carrots, chopped
2 celery stalks, chopped
14 ounces canned plum tomatoes
4 ounces cavolo nero or cabbage, shredded
1 red chile pepper
1 teaspoon chopped fresh oregano or ½ teaspoon dried
1 teaspoon chopped fresh rosemary (or ½ teaspoon dried)

8 cups miso broth (see page 150) or good quality vegetable stock (see page 151)
⅓–½ cup dry white wine (optional)
Freshly ground sea salt and black pepper
8 thin slices of good quality crusty whole-wheat bread
4 garlic cloves
1 teaspoon chopped fresh thyme or ½ teaspoon dried
1 red onion, thinly sliced
1 cup Parmesan cheese, freshly grated

Serves 6–8

Soak the beans in water to cover generously. Leave overnight. Next day, drain and rinse the beans well. In a large heavy-bottomed saucepan, heat two tablespoons of the oil and sauté the onion in it briefly until just translucent, then add the vegetables, chile pepper, oregano, and rosemary. Sauté for about five minutes, until all the vegetables are well coated in the oil and beginning to soften. Add the beans and mix in to coat them well.

Add the miso broth or vegetable stock and the wine. Bring to the boil, lower the heat and simmer for about one and a half hours, until the beans are quite soft. Season to taste (don't add salt before this point or the beans' skins will harden). Allow to cool slightly and take out the chile pepper.

Preheat the oven to 350°F. Ladle out about half the contents of the saucepan (try to favor the beans and leave the vegetables) and puree in a food processor or with a food mill. Return to the saucepan and mix well.

Rub the bread with one or two garlic cloves and toast. Finely chop the remaining garlic. Heat the remaining oil and gently sauté the garlic with the thyme and lots of black pepper, until softened and aromatic. Stir into the soup and season.

Pour about half the saucepan's contents into an ovenproof casserole, spread the toasted bread over that and then empty the rest of the pan's contents on top. Arrange the slices of red onion over the top, and scatter with the cheese.

Bake in the oven for about 30 minutes, until the top is golden.

P **** E * A ***
PHYTOESTROGENS IN ABUNDANCE FROM THE MIX OF VEGETABLES AND BEANS. THE CARROTS AND TOMATOES CONTAIN HIGH LEVELS OF ANTIOXIDANTS.

thai mushroom noodle soup

The many health benefits of shiitake mushrooms include protection against heart disease and cancer. Ginger is excellent for increasing the circulation and has traditionally been used for reducing inflammation in the joints and helping arthritis. It can also help with nausea, which is common during menopause.

1 ounce dried shiitake or other mushrooms
⅔ cup boiling water
6 ounces fresh chestnut mushrooms
Bunch of scallions
4½ cups miso broth (see page 150)
2 tablespoons tom yum soup paste
1 tablespoon soy sauce

½ small red chile, thinly sliced (optional)
1-inch piece of ginger root, peeled and grated
2 garlic cloves, thinly sliced
2 tablespoons no-added-sugar fish sauce
3 ounces egg thread noodles
6 ounces spinach or beansprouts, shredded
7 ounces tofu, diced

Serves 4

First soak the dried mushrooms in the boiling water for about 10 minutes. Drain them, reserving the liquid. Then slice the chestnut mushrooms and scallions.

Bring the miso broth and reserved mushroom liquid almost to a boil, then stir in the tom yum soup paste. Add the sliced mushrooms, reserved shiitake mushrooms, scallions, soy sauce, chile (if using), ginger, garlic, and fish sauce. Simmer for about 10 minutes.

Add the noodles, spinach, and tofu to the soup, and cook for a further three to five minutes, until the noodles are just tender. To serve, divide the soup and noodles between warmed serving bowls.

P **** E ** A *

PHYTOESTROGENS ARE PRESENT IN THE SHIITAKE MUSHROOMS, TOFU, BEANSPROUTS, MISO BROTH, AND GARLIC.

carrot and cilantro soup

Carrot and cilantro is a favorite combination for many people – and rightly so. They complement each other beautifully. Water, miso broth, or vegetable broth can be used as a base for the soup; obviously, if you use broth it will have a deeper flavor, but the soup is still delicious made with just water.

1 pound, 2 ounces baby carrots, chopped small
1 large onion, chopped small
2 garlic cloves
Grated peeland juice of 1 unwaxed orange
1 teaspoon ground coriander seeds
Large handful of cilantro, with roots, plus more sprigs for garnishing

2½ cups boiling water, miso broth (see page 150) or vegetable stock (see page 151)
1¼ cups soy milk
Freshly ground sea salt and black pepper
2 teaspoons honey
⅓–½ cup tofu cream (see page 155), thick unset plain yogurt, preferably soy yogurt, or heavy cream (optional)

Serves 4

Put the carrots, onion, garlic, orange peel, and ground coriander in a large heavy pot with the cilantro stalks and roots tied together by a couple of stalks. Add the water, broth, and soy milk, and bring to a simmer. Cook gently for about 30 minutes until everything is quite tender.

Transfer to a food processor or blender with most of the cilantro leaves and the orange juice, and puree. Pour and spoon back into the rinsed-out pan, taste and adjust the seasoning with salt, pepper, and honey.

Stir in the tofu cream, yogurt, or cream, if using it, and heat through gently, stirring. Scatter over the reserved cilantro leaves before serving.

P **** E * A ****

PHYTOESTROGENS FROM THE MISO BROTH, TOFU CREAM OR SOY YOGURT, SOY MILK, AND GARLIC. THE CARROTS CONTAIN THE ANTIOXIDANT BETA-CAROTENE.

minestrone primavera

Because of its great number of vegetables, minestrone is an excellent soup for obtaining a good variety of phytoestrogens. Zucchini are an excellent source of beta-carotene, vitamin C, and folic acid. The cabbage offers effective anti-cancer protection by helping estrogen to be excreted in its harmless form.

⅓ cup dried cannellini beans
⅓ cup borlotti beans
2 tablespoons olive oil
1½ ounces mixed seaweed flakes
1 large onion, chopped
1 garlic clove, chopped
1 bay leaf
3 baby leeks, cut into small bite-sized chunks
6 ounces young carrots, cut into small bite-sized chunks
3–4 celery hearts, cut into small bite-sized chunks
6 ounces young zucchini, diced large
6 ounces fine green beans, cut into small bite-sized lengths
½ cup shelled peas
6 ¼ cups boiling water, miso broth (see page 150)
　or vegetable stock (see page 151)
2 tablespoons red wine
6 ounces young spring cabbage, finely shredded
6 ounces new potatoes, cut in half
8 ounces tomatoes, skinned (see page 58) and coarsely chopped
Freshly ground sea salt and black pepper
¾ cup soup pasta, such as ditalini or vermicelli
3 tablespoons chopped flat-leaf parsley
Handful of basil
Garlic croutons (see page 60), to serve
Freshly grated Parmesan cheese, to serve

Serves 6–8

Cover the beans generously with water and leave to soak overnight. The next day, drain and rinse them well.

Heat the oil in a large heavy-bottomed pot and add the seaweed. Sauté gently for a minute or so, then add the onion, garlic clove, and the bay leaf, and continue to sauté gently for about five minutes. Then add the leeks, carrots, and celery and cook for two to three minutes more. Drain both soaked beans and add them to the pan. Sauté for about five minutes more. Add the zucchini, green beans, and peas, and sauté for another five minutes.

Add the water or broth, together with the wine, cabbage, potatoes, and tomatoes. Bring to the boil, cover and simmer very gently for about 1¾–2 hours, until the beans are tender. Season to taste, crumble in the pasta, add the parsley and basil, and continue to cook for about 10–15 minutes, until the pasta is tender.

Serve the soup with bowls of the croutons and the grated Parmesan. You could also dress the finished soup with a big dollop of pesto sauce (see page 154).

P ***** E * A ***
PHYTOESTROGENS IN THE MISO BROTH, CANNELLINI AND BORLOTTI BEANS, CELERY, CARROTS, PEAS, GREEN BEANS, POTATOES, AND GARLIC.

salade niçoise

This delicious dish is supremely good for your well-being. Good quantities of monounsaturated oils are available from the black olives and the olive oil in the dressing. Eggs are an excellent healthy source of protein and are full of nutrients, especially the B vitamins (the "anti-stress" vitamins) and zinc (essential for hormone balance and healthy bones).

8 ounces small new potatoes
6 ounces fine green beans
2–3 eggs
1 Romaine lettuce or 2 Romaine hearts
Small bunch of scallions
½ English cucumber
2 medium tomatoes
1 red pepper
1 large can (7 ounces) of tuna chunks in oil
About 1 cup anchovy fillets, rinsed and drained
1 cup pitted black olives, preferably garlic-flavored
Several handfuls of fresh herbs, particularly flat-leaf parsley, chives, basil, chervil, and tarragon

For the dressing
1 garlic clove
3 tablespoons extra virgin olive oil
2 tablespoons linseed oil
1 tablespoon balsamic vinegar
Freshly ground sea salt and black pepper

Serves 4–6

Put a pan of salted water on to heat. Scrub the potatoes or peel only if absolutely necessary. When the water is boiling, add the beans and blanch for one or two minutes only. Remove with a slotted spoon and drop into a bowl of cold water.

Add the potatoes to the boiling water and cook them at a good simmer until barely tender – they must not become mushy. Put another pan of water on to heat and add the eggs. They should be boiled for 12 minutes only and no more.

While the potatoes and eggs are cooking, prepare the other fresh vegetables. Shred the lettuce leaves into the bottom of a large salad bowl. Trim the scallions and snip them over the leaves. Slice the cucumber lengthwise into two or three long slices and then cut these into long strips; finally cut across into three-quarter inch chunks. Quarter the tomatoes and cut the quarters in half again if large. Cut the pepper in half and seed it, then slice the flesh across into thinnish strips. Add all these to the bowl. Drain the tuna and flake in half of it at this stage. Using scissors, snip in half the anchovies and add half the olives. Snip in half the herbs.

By this time the potatoes should be cooked and the eggs hard-boiled. Drain and dry the potatoes briefly over a very low heat, then leave to cool slightly on a flat plate. Drain the eggs and dunk them in cold water. Pour off the water from the cooled beans and drain on paper towels.

Make the dressing: crush the garlic into the mixed oils, add the vinegar, and season with salt and pepper to taste. Mix well into a smooth emulsion and adjust the seasoning.

Cut the potatoes into bite-sized chunks if necessary and add these to the salad, together with the beans. Pour the dressing over the salad and toss well to mix. At this stage taste and adjust the seasoning.

Shell the eggs, cut into quarters and arrange over the top of the salad, together with the remaining tuna, olives, and anchovies. Snip over the herbs.

P ** E ***** A ***
PHYTOESTROGENS IN THE POTATOES, GREEN BEANS, AND HERBS (ESPECIALLY PARSLEY AND SAGE). EFAS AS OMEGA 3 IN THE ANCHOVIES AND TUNA.

mushroom crostini

This irresistible appetizer smells and tastes luxurious and is good for you – garlic and shallots are excellent for the immune system and garlic is particularly effective against tumors.

1½ ounces dried porcini
  mushrooms
1 tablespoon olive oil
Pat of butter
2 shallots, finely chopped
2 garlic cloves, crushed
1 teaspoon finely chopped
  fresh sage

Dash of balsamic vinegar
5 ounces chestnut mushrooms
Small handful of flat-leaf parsley,
  plus more for garnishing
Freshly ground sea salt and
  black pepper
1 ciabatta loaf, cut into 4
  lengths and each piece cut
  across in half

Serves 4

Rinse the dried mushrooms carefully in cold running water, then soak them in a bowl of warm water for about 20 minutes. Pat them dry and chop them coarsely. Strain the soaking water and set aside.

Heat the oil and butter in a wide-based skillet and sauté the shallots until translucent. Add the garlic, sauté briefly, then add the reconstituted mushrooms with two-thirds cup of the strained soaking liquid plus the sage and vinegar. Cover and cook over a gentle heat for about 15 minutes.

Wipe the fresh mushrooms clean with paper towels. Slice them not too thinly. Turn the heat up and add them to the pan with the parsley, reserving a few sprigs for garnishing. Cook over medium to high heat for 5–7 minutes uncovered, stirring occasionally, until most of the liquid has evaporated. Season.

Toast the slices of bread and spread the mushroom mixture on top. Garnish with the reserved parsley.

Variation: make this into a more substantial snack by adding a layer of cheese, such as mozzarella or grated Parmesan.

P ** E * A *
PHYTOESTROGENS ARE CONTAINED IN THE MUSHROOMS, SAGE, GARLIC, PARSLEY, AND BREAD.

crab and avocado salad

Crab contains zinc and magnesium as well as selenium, which is anti-aging and cancer-protective. Avocados have been shown to help produce collagen, which is important for maintaining healthy skin and bones. They also have high amounts of the mineral potassium, which helps prevent water retention.

1 large avocado, preferably Hass
Juice of 1 lemon
7 ounces dressed fresh crab
  meat (brown and white) –
  about 2 cups
½ teaspoon anchovy paste
½ teaspoon mustard powder
2 tablespoons golden flax seeds

Freshly ground sea salt
  and black pepper
2 large eggs, hard-boiled,
  shelled, and chopped
3 tablespoons mayonnaise
  (ready-made or see
  page 153)
Mixed soft salad leaves,
  for serving

Serves 4

Peel and cut in half the avocado, then pit and dice it. Toss the pieces in the juice of half the lemon.

Pick over the crab meat to remove any residual pieces of shell. Put the brown meat in one bowl and flake the white into another. Into the brown meat, mix the remaining lemon juice, the anchovy paste, mustard powder, and flax seeds, with seasoning to taste, Into the white flesh, gently mix the egg and the mayonnaise with any remaining lemon juice drained from the avocado and some seasoning. Arrange the salad leaves on serving plates. There are two ways of serving this: either combine the contents of both bowls together with the avocado dice and spoon mounds of this on top of the salad; or arrange in layers, with the avocado on top of the leaves, followed by the brown meat and then the white. Layering inside a round pastry cutter helps give a neat and attractive shape.

P *** E *** A ***
PHYTOESTROGENS FROM THE LINSEEDS AND CRAB. ANTIOXIDANTS IN THE AVOCADO AND CRAB. EFAS FROM THE LINSEEDS.

piedmontese peppers with anchovies

Perhaps surprisingly, peppers can contain twice as much vitamin C as oranges. Vitamin C is vital for the bones as it produces collagen. The herb basil is noted for its tranquilizing effect on the body – important at the menopause when our moods can fluctuate – and oregano is good for the digestion.

4 red or yellow peppers
4 garlic cloves, sliced
½ cup pitted black olives, chopped
4 anchovy fillets, rinsed, drained, and chopped
1 tablespoon capers, rinsed and drained
4 plum tomatoes, cut in half
3 tablespoons extra virgin olive oil, plus more for greasing
Freshly ground sea salt and black pepper
Large handful of fresh basil, roughly chopped
2 tablespoons fresh oregano, roughly chopped

Serves 4

Preheat the oven to 425°F. Cut the peppers in half and remove the seeds but not the stalks. Place the peppers skin-side down on a lightly oiled baking sheet.

Place slices of garlic inside each pepper half, scatter with the olive and anchovy pieces and the capers, then top each with a plum tomato half, cut-side down. Drizzle with the oil, season, and bake for 10 minutes.

Reduce the oven setting to 400°F and continue baking for a further 15–20 minutes, until the peppers and tomatoes are tender.

Serve the peppers hot or cold, scattered with the fresh herbs.

P ** E *** A ****
PHYTOESTROGENS PROVIDED BY THE GARLIC AND PEPPERS. ANCHOVIES CONTAIN EFAS IN THE FORM OF OMEGA 3 OILS.

shrimp and sesame toasts

Shrimp are a good source of vitamin B12, but as this is a fried dish, keep it for special treats only. Buy fresh firm shrimp, rinse them well and pat them quite dry with paper towels. If using frozen shrimp, make sure they are well defrosted and drained – you will also need about twice the weight of fresh shrimp.

4 scallions
8 ounces cooked shrimp, peeled (about 2 cups)
Small sprig of cilantro, plus more leaves for garnishing (optional)
¾-inch piece of fresh ginger root, peeled and crushed in a garlic press
2 teaspoons cornstarch
½ teaspoon honey
2 teaspoons light soy sauce
1 teaspoon dry sherry
Good dash of Tabasco (optional)
½ teaspoon dark sesame oil
1 egg
Freshly ground sea salt and black pepper
Olive oil, for frying
12 thin slices of day-old whole-wheat bread, crusts removed
4 tablespoons sesame seeds
Lime wedges, to serve (optional)

Serves 4 (makes about 48)

Coarsely snip the scallions into the bowl of a food processor. Add the shrimp, cilantro, ginger (all the juice and bits included), cornstarch, honey, soy sauce, sherry, Tabasco to taste (if using), and the sesame oil, and process until the scallions and shrimp are finely chopped.

Add the egg, season generously with salt and pepper to taste, and then process again briefly until the mixture forms a smoothish paste.

Pour the olive oil into a wok or large skillet to a depth of about a half inch and heat to the point where a small cube of the bread will brown in about 40 seconds.

While the oil is heating, spread each slice of bread with some of the shrimp mixture. Sprinkle the tops with sesame seeds.

Cut each slice of bread into four triangles or long strips. Fry the strips in batches, paste side down, for about one minute and then turn them over and fry the other side very briefly (about 15–20 seconds), until the toasts are a uniform golden brown. As soon as each batch is cooked, remove from the skillet, drain them on layers of paper towels and keep in a warm place, uncovered.

Serve as soon as all are cooked with lime wedges on the side and garnished with some more cilantro if you like.

Variations: vary the flavor of the shrimp mixture by using parsley instead of cilantro and/or replacing the ginger with some chopped seaweed.

P* E** A*
PHYTOESTROGENS FROM THE WHOLE-WHEAT BREAD AND SESAME SEEDS AND PARSLEY, IF USED. SHRIMP CONTAIN THE POWERFUL ANTIOXIDANT, SELENIUM.

moroccan carrot and orange salad

You could call this the Moroccan Antioxidant Salad just from its glorious color. An ideal summer appetizer, this salad makes a fine accompaniment to spicy vegetable and grain dishes and strongly flavored fish dishes. Adding tofu to the salad would mean that the phytoestrogen content is increased from *** to ****.

2 large juicy navel oranges
12 ounces baby carrots
1 head of endive
Pinch of cinnamon or 1 tablespoon orange flower water (optional)
For the dressing
1 tablespoon clear honey

2 tablespoons extra virgin olive oil
1 tablespoon flax seed oil
1 tablespoon golden linseeds
1 tablespoon lemon juice
2 tablespoons cilantro, finely chopped (optional)
Freshly ground sea salt and black pepper

Serves 4

Peel the orange, removing as much of the white pith as you can. Using a sharp knife, slice the fruit horizontally into very thin round slices and then cut these in half, reserving the resulting juices for the dressing.

Scrub the carrots and pare them into long shreds. Trim the endive of its base and discard the outer leaves. Separate the inner leaves. Place the shredded carrots, chicory leaves, and orange slices in a salad bowl. Chill briefly.

Just before serving, beat the dressing ingredients together with the reserved orange juice until they are well blended. Season to taste. Pour the dressing over the salad and toss carefully until well coated. Sprinkle over some cinnamon or orange flower water if you like.

Variation: this salad is also good sprinkled with some lightly toasted pine nuts. You could also toss in a few cubes of tofu to create an excellent light meal or snack.

P *** E *** A *****
BETA-CAROTENE, FROM THE ORANGE FRUITS AND VEGETABLES. PHYTOESTROGENS FROM THE CARROTS AND FLAX SEEDS. EFAS FROM THE FLAX SEEDS.

guacamole

Avocados may be high in calories, but they come in the form of the beneficial monounsaturated fats, which are exceptionally easy to digest. Avocados are high in potassium, which helps prevent water retention, and are also a rich source of vitamin E and vitamin C, B6, riboflavin, and manganese. They have also been found to help produce collagen.

4 scallions
Large handful of cilantro leaves
Grated peel and juice of 2 limes
3 large ripe avocados (Hass if available)
2 small red chiles, seeded and thinly sliced
1 pound, 2 ounces very ripe tomatoes, skinned (see page 58), stalk ends removed and finely chopped
Freshly ground sea salt and black pepper

Serves 4

Coarsely chop the scallions into the bowl of a food processor and add all but a few sprigs of the cilantro, the peel and juice of the limes, and the flesh of two of the avocados. Puree.

Add the remaining avocado, the chile and all but a few spoonfuls of the tomatoes and pulse gently until the avocado flesh is broken up but there are still visible small chunks of it. Do not over-process. Season to taste with salt and pepper.

Pour into serving bowls, spoon a little of the reserved chopped tomato into the center of each bowl and top with a reserved cilantro leaf. It is traditional to serve this Mexican dip with corn chips, but it is just as nice – and healthier – accompanied by vegetable crudités.

P * E ** A ****
TOMATOES CONTAIN THE ANTIOXIDANT LYCOPENE, WHICH HELPS COUNTER CELL DAMAGE AND PREMATURE AGING.

hummus bi tahini

This is one of my favorite dishes for menopause because it is extremely good for us. The olives and olive oil are good for lowering cholesterol and helping the heart. The sesame seeds contain high amounts of calcium. Hummus is delicious as a dip with pita, or as a sauce for roasted vegetables or fish.

1 pound chickpeas or 2 large 14-ounce cans of cooked chickpeas, drained
4 large garlic cloves
2 hot red chiles
Juice of about 3 lemons
About ⅔ cup tahini paste

¾ cup pitted black olives, plus a few for garnishing
2 teaspoons ground cumin
About 1 teaspoon freshly ground sea salt
Extra virgin olive oil, to dress
A little paprika, to garnish
Chopped flat-leaf parsley, for garnishing
Warm pita bread, for serving

Serves 6–8

If using dried chickpeas, soak them overnight in water. Next day, discard the water, cover with fresh cold water and bring to a boil. Lower the heat, add one of the garlic cloves and the chiles and simmer for one hour, until just soft. Drain, reserving the water and discarding the garlic and chiles.

Reserving a few whole chickpeas, put the rest in a food processor with the lemon juice, tahini paste, olives, cumin, two-thirds cup of the reserved water (or plain water or miso broth, see page 150, if using canned chickpeas) and salt. Chop the remaining garlic, add to the processor and puree. The consistency should not be too smooth, with discernible pieces of chickpeas giving texture. Add more water if too dry. Adjust the flavoring with more tahini, lemon juice, and salt to taste.

Spread the hummus on individual plates, forking circular ridges on the surface. Pour a little olive oil over, arrange a few whole chickpeas and olives on top, dust with a little paprika and garnish with the parsley. Serve with warm pita bread.

P ***** E ***** A **
CHICKPEAS CONTAIN ALL FOUR ISOFLAVONES (IMPORTANT PHYTOESTROGENS). EFAS ARE SUPPLIED BY THE SESAME SEEDS AND OLIVE OIL.

3

lunches and light meals

zucchini risotto

This risotto is fantastic with really fresh firm young zucchini. Zucchini are rich in vitamin C and folic acid, and one serving of this delicious dish provides you with more than a quarter of your daily needs of vitamin C.

8 cups miso broth (see page 150) or good quality vegetable stock (see page 151)
6 tablespoons butter
2 tablespoons olive oil
1 onion, diced
1½ cups risotto rice (such as arborio)
4 tablespoons dry white wine (optional)
Freshly ground sea salt and black pepper
1 pound zucchini, sliced at an angle and not too thinly
1 cup grated Parmesan cheese

Serves 4

Heat the miso or vegetable broth, and when it is almost boiling turn the heat down and keep it at a very gentle simmer. Heat half the butter with the oil in a heavy-bottomed pot and fry the onion until translucent. Add the rice and stir for a minute or two until every grain is coated and shiny with oil and butter. Add the wine if using, and allow to boil off, stirring. Then add the broth a ladleful at a time, stirring it in and not adding the next ladleful until it is well absorbed.

After about 10 minutes, season and add the zucchini. Continue adding the broth and stirring. Taste after 20 minutes. The rice should have a discernible bite and the texture of the risotto should be thick and porridge-like. If you have used up the broth but the rice is not done, finish with ladlefuls of boiling water.

Remove the risotto from the heat, stir in the remaining butter and the cheese, cover, and leave to stand for three minutes. Serve immediately. For a special-occasion dish, add a good pinch of saffron strands to the broth and add some shredded basil leaves at the end with the butter and cheese.

P *** E * A ***
THE MISO BROTH GIVES YOU A GOOD AMOUNT OF PHYTOESTROGENS AND THE ZUCCHINI ARE AN EXCELLENT SOURCE OF THE ANTIOXIDANT BETA-CAROTENE.

mozzarella and tomato gratin

Insalata tricolore remains an irresistible favorite for many food lovers; this dish takes that wonderful combination of mozzarella, tomato, and basil and makes it even more tempting, by melting the cheese. The olives are valuable for their beneficial effects on the heart.

12 ounces vine-ripened tomatoes, sliced
Freshly ground sea salt and black pepper
Handful of basil, shredded, plus more sprigs for garnishing
2 tablespoons pitted black olives, cut into slivers
2 tablespoons pine nuts
3 fresh (preferably buffalo) mozzarella cheeses, each about 3½ ounces, cut into slices
Balsamic vinegar

Serves 4

Preheat a hot broiler. Arrange the tomato slices in the bottom of a medium-sized gratin dish and season well. Sprinkle over the shredded basil, olive slivers, and half the pine nuts.

Arrange the cheese slices over the top and sprinkle over the remaining pine nuts and a few drops of balsamic vinegar here and there. Season again with pepper.

Broil until the mozzarella is nicely melted and the bottom of the dish is good and hot.

Serve at once, garnished with the reserved sprigs of basil.

Variation: for a more substantial dish, try adding some rinsed and drained anchovy fillets to the layer between the tomatoes and the cheese. They add a more sophisticated flavor. The gratin is also delicious served on thick slices of ciabatta bread instead of in the dish, to make crostini.

P * E * A ***
TOMATOES PROVIDE THE ANTIOXIDANT LYCOPENE, WHICH MAY HELP TO PREVENT AGAINST CANCER, HEART DISEASE, AND DEGENERATIVE EYE CONDITIONS.

pasta with crushed nut vinaigrette

The interesting nutty flavor that infuses this pasta belies its simplicity. From the flax seeds and whole-wheat pasta you will get phytoestrogens, plus gain benefits for your heart from the olive oil. Walnuts are rich in essential fatty acids and so are especially good for the heart and joints.

Freshly ground sea salt and black pepper
1 pound (preferably whole-wheat) pasta shapes, such as shells or spirals
1 cup grated Parmesan cheese, to serve
For the crushed nut vinaigrette
2 tablespoons extra virgin olive oil
1 tablespoon flaxseed oil
2 teaspoons balsamic vinegar
¾ cup shelled walnuts, coarsely chopped or crushed

Serves 4

Fill a large saucepan with water and bring to a boil. Salt and add the pasta. Cook, stirring occasionally, until the pasta is *al dente*, i.e., soft but still offering some resistance when you bite it.

While the pasta is cooking, make the vinaigrette: whisk all the ingredients together well (or shake to an emulsion in a sealed jar), reserving about a tablespoon of the chopped nuts for garnish and adding seasoning to taste.

Drain the pasta well, pour over the vinaigrette, and toss to coat well. Serve immediately, garnished with the reserved nuts and some Parmesan, along with the rest of the grated cheese served in a bowl.

P *** E *** A *
PHYTOESTROGENS ARE PROVIDED BY THE FLAX SEEDS AND WHOLE-WHEAT PASTA. WALNUTS CONTAIN ESSENTIAL FATTY ACIDS.

pasta with broccoli and anchovies

A simple but delicious combination of ingredients. Anchovies contain Omega 3 oils, which are good for the heart and the skin and joints. The broccoli helps to guard against cancer as it contains beta-carotene and vitamins K and C. Choose dark florets as the richer the color, the more nutrients it contains.

Freshly ground sea salt and black pepper
4 cups (preferably whole-wheat) pasta noodles, such as tagliatelle
1 pound broccoli, cut into bite-sized pieces (about 8 cups)
3 tablespoons olive oil
6 garlic cloves, thinly sliced
4–6 anchovy fillets, rinsed, drained, and chopped
Grated Parmesan cheese, for serving

Serves 4

Cook the pasta as described in the previous recipe. While the pasta is cooking, bring a large saucepan of salted water to the boil. Blanch the broccoli in the boiling water for one minute only after it comes back to a boil. Drain, refresh in cold water to stop it cooking any more, and drain well.

Heat the oil in a large skillet until almost hot and add the garlic. Sauté until just turning golden-brown in color. Add the broccoli and anchovies with seasoning and sauté for a minute or two more.

Drain the cooked pasta well and either return to the pan or put in a large warmed serving bowl. Pour over the contents of the skillet, adding more seasoning if necessary, and toss well. Serve accompanied by the cheese.

P ** E *** A *
ANCHOVIES ARE AN EXCELLENT SOURCE OF OMEGA 3 ESSENTIAL FATTY ACIDS; THE WHOLE-WHEAT PASTA PROVIDES THE NECESSARY PHYTOESTROGENS.

pasta salad primavera

All the spring vegetables in this pasta combine to offer good phytoestrogens, especially the carrots, peas, green beans, and the parsley. The whole-wheat pasta is also a good source of phytoestrogens. The tomatoes and zucchini supply plenty of antioxidants and the essential oils are covered by the flaxseed oil.

Freshly ground sea salt and black pepper
2 cups (preferably whole-wheat) pasta shapes, such as penne, spirals, bows, or shells, or a mixture
6 baby carrots, whole or halved lengthwise if thick
4 ounces fine green beans
6 baby zucchini, cut in half lengthwise
1 tablespoon butter
4 ounces snow peas, cut into strips if large
4 scallions, quartered at an angle
4 ounces (roughly 8–10) cherry tomatoes (preferably Santa baby plum tomatoes), cut in half
½ cup pitted whole black olives
1 cup Parmesan cheese

For the parsley vinaigrette
3 tablespoons olive oil
2 tablespoons flaxseed oil
1 tablespoon balsamic vinegar
1 tablespoon fresh parsley, chopped

Serves 4

Cook the pasta as for the Pasta with Crushed Nut Vinaigrette (see page 76).

While the pasta is cooking, make the vinaigrette: whisk all the ingredients together well (or shake to an emulsion in a sealed jar), adding seasoning to taste.

Drain the cooked pasta well, pour over half the vinaigrette and toss well to coat thoroughly, then leave to cool.

Meanwhile, prepare the vegetables: in separate small pans of boiling salted water cook the carrots, beans, and zucchini until just tender. As they are done, drain, refresh in cold water, and drain again.

Melt the butter in a skillet over low-to-medium heat and sauté the snow peas and scallions until just beginning to wilt. Add all the remaining vegetables and toss to coat.

Transfer to a serving bowl, add half the olives and the remaining vinaigrette and toss to coat, then mix in the pasta. Dot with the remaining olives and with long shavings of the Parmesan made using a swivel peeler.

P *** E *** A ***
PHYTOESTROGENS IN THE FORM OF SPRING VEGETABLES, ANTIOXIDANTS ARE SUPPLIED BY THE TOMATOES AND ZUCCHINI, EFAS FROM THE FLAXSEED OIL.

pasta with fried sage leaves

This is another simple but fresh-tasting pasta dish that uses a healthy combination of foods. It uses an excellent herb for menopause, sage, which is known to help reduce hot flashes. You are provided with phytoestrogens from the whole-wheat pasta and the pine nuts.

Freshly ground sea salt and black pepper
4 cups pasta noodles, such as tagliatelle (preferably whole-wheat)
2 tablespoons olive oil
2 tablespoons butter
Large handful of sage
½ cup pine nuts
1 cup grated Parmesan cheese, plus more to serve

Serves 4

Cook the pasta as for the Pasta with Crushed Nut Vinaigrette (see page 76).

While the pasta is cooking, heat the oil and butter in a large skillet and fry half the sage leaves on both sides until crisp. Remove from the saucepan with tongs, and drain on a layer of paper towels. Add the pine nuts to the saucepan and sauté until golden. Finely chop the remaining sage and stir into the pine nuts.

Drain the cooked pasta well and either return to the saucepan or put in a large warmed serving bowl. Pour over the contents of the skillet, add the Parmesan, and season to taste.

Toss with the whole sage leaves to serve, accompanied by more grated cheese.

P *** E ** A *
THE WHOLE-WHEAT PASTA AND THE PINE NUTS OFFER PHYTOESTROGENS.
THE PINE NUTS ALSO CONTAIN ESSENTIAL OILS.

refried bean tortillas with tomato salsa

Onions are known to help prevent osteoporosis and the garlic is reported to have anti-cancer effects. The limes are an excellent source of vitamin C, which helps to combat free radicals and prevent premature aging. For a party dish, cut the tortillas into small wedges and spread the beans on them.

6 tablespoons olive oil
1 pound cooked (or canned) pinto beans or red kidney beans
Freshly ground sea salt and black pepper
3–4 tablespoons hot miso broth (see page 150)
4–6 scallions, chopped
1½ cups Cheddar cheese, grated
8 corn tortillas or 4 flour tortillas
1 Romaine lettuce heart, shredded

For the tomato salsa
6 large ripe but firm tomatoes, preferably plum or vine
1 red onion, diced
1 garlic clove, very finely chopped
1 large red pepper, seeded and diced
1–2 red chiles, seeded and chopped
Juice of 2 limes
Large handful of cilantro, chopped, plus some whole leaves
   for garnishing
Freshly ground sea salt and black pepper

Serves 4

First make the salsa: cut the tomatoes in half, and scoop out and discard the seeds. Dice the flesh (skin included) and put it in a serving bowl, together with the red onion, garlic, pepper, chile, lime juice, chopped cilantro, and seasoning. Mix well, cover, and chill while you fry the beans.

Heat half the oil in a large skillet and add the beans (you will need to drain them if they are canned). Season and, if they are very dry, add a few spoonfuls of the hot miso broth. Fry the beans briskly, stirring frequently with a wooden spoon.

As the beans soften, start to press them down with the spoon to form a large cake and keep cooking until the cake is glazed and will move as one piece in the pan.

Move this to one side of the pan and turn it over like a pancake, then cook the other side in the same way. Turn off the heat under the skillet and sprinkle the beans with the scallions followed by the cheese. Cover.

At the same time, cook the tortillas: heat the remaining oil in a skillet and, when it is hot, dip each of the tortillas into it, one at a time, for about 15 seconds each.

Once the cheese has melted, serve the refried beans on a bed of shredded lettuce with the tortillas (break flour tortillas into pieces) and the salsa in separate bowls.

Variation: for an even more substantial and phyto-packed version of this dish, sprinkle some bite-sized pieces of cooked broccoli on top of the beans with the scallions. It is delicious served with guacamole (see page 71).

P ***** E * A *****
REFRIED BEAN TORTILLAS ARE PACKED WITH PHYTOESTROGENS FROM THE BEANS, MISO, GARLIC, AND CORN. THE TOMATOES AND PEPPER PROVIDE ANTIOXIDANTS.

tofu vegetable quiche

This quiche is an unusual way to serve tofu and makes an interesting change. Made from sesame seeds, the tahini is also a rich source of calcium. Healthfood stores should sell pre-baked savory tart shells; otherwise use an ordinary pastry tart suitable for quiche, but make sure it is made with whole-wheat flour.

2 tablespoons tahini
3 tablespoons soy sauce
2 pounds soft tofu, mashed
1 tablespoon arrowroot
1 pound broccoli, cut into small bite-sized pieces (about 8 cups)
1 pre-baked savory tart shell

Serves 4

Preheat the oven to 300°F.

Combine the tahini, soy sauce, and the tofu in a bowl. Dissolve the arrowroot in three fluid ounces water and combine with the tahini mixture in a saucepan. Bring to a simmer and continue to cook over medium heat for 7–10 minutes.

Meanwhile, in a separate pan, steam the broccoli pieces until they are just beginning to get tender. Add the broccoli to the tofu mixture and spoon into the pie shell. Bake in the preheated oven for eight minutes.

P **** E ** A **
THE TOFU, TAHINI, AND BROCCOLI ALL DELIVER PHYTOESTROGENS. EFAS ARE PROVIDED BY THE SESAME SEEDS.

russian salad deluxe with tofu dressing

This salad is truly deluxe as it has such an interesting variety of vegetables. The mix of colors provided by the green peas, orange carrots, red beets, black and green grapes, and the apples gives plenty of different and important antioxidants.

3 ounces waxy potatoes, peeled
3 ounces baby carrots, scrubbed
3 ounces peas
3 ounces cooked beets, peeled
½ fennel bulb, cored and finely chopped, fronds reserved for garnishing
3 ounces grapes (black and green), cut in half and seeded
2 large eating apples, cored and diced (leave skin on)

Serves 4

¾ cup walnuts
2 ounces capers
Romaine heart lettuces, shredded, to serve

For the tofu dressing
9 ounces tofu
3 tablespoons cider vinegar
2 tablespoons olive oil
1 tablespoon flaxseed oil
1 tablespoon soy sauce
Freshly ground sea salt and black pepper

Cook the potatoes, carrots, and peas in separate saucepans of boiling salted water until just tender. Drain well and, when cool, cut the potatoes and carrots into half-inch cubes. Cut the beets into the same sized cubes.

Put all these in a large, preferably glass, salad bowl together with the fennel, grapes (reserving a few of each color for garnish), apples, walnuts, and capers. Toss lightly to mix.

Make the dressing: blend all the ingredients in a food processor until smooth. Season to taste. Spoon over the salad and toss so that all the ingredients are lightly coated but are still identifiable.

Serve on beds of shredded lettuce, garnished with fennel fronds and more grape halves.

P ***** E **** A *****
A SUPERB MIX OF PHYTOESTROGENS FROM THE TOFU, FENNEL, CARROTS, PEAS, AND APPLES. EFAS FROM THE FLAXSEED OIL AND THE WALNUTS.

gado gado salad

Indonesian gado gado is an unusual combination of hot and cold ingredients. Although we don't want to eat a lot of fried food, the occasional fried tofu and so on is fine as long as it is balanced with other ingredients. The cauliflower, watercress, and carrots are excellent sources of vitamin C.

About 1¾ cups peanut sauce (see page 155), reheated if necessary
7 ounces tofu, cut into ½-inch slices
1 tablespoon olive oil

For the salad
4–6 carrots, cut into matchstick strips
6 ounces beansprouts
6 ounces fine green beans
4 ounces cauliflower florets
1 tablespoon linseeds

Serves 4–6

1 small head of Chinese leaves, thinly sliced

For the garnish
½ cucumber, cut into thickish matchstick strips
4 hard-boiled eggs, cut into wedges
4 cooked potatoes, cut into wedges
Large handful of watercress or baby spinach
1 large onion, sliced and dry-fried until crisp
Large handful of no-added-sugar shrimp crackers

First make the peanut sauce (see page 155). Keep warm. Then sauté the tofu in a little olive oil, until it is crunchy.

Combine this and all the other salad ingredients (you can either serve this dish in individual portions or in one big bowl). Pour the warm peanut sauce over the salad, then arrange the garnish ingredients: place the cucumber, egg, and potato around the edge and pile the watercress or spinach and dry-fried onions in the center.

Serve immediately, sprinkled with the no-added-sugar shrimp crackers.

P **** E *** A *****
THE TOFU IS VERY HIGH IN PHYTOESTROGENS AND SO ARE THE BEANSPROUTS. ANTIOXIDANTS ARE PROVIDED BY THE WATERCRESS, CARROTS, AND CUCUMBERS.

broiled sardines with fennel and pine nuts

The sardines and pine nuts are so beneficial for the skin and joints, garlic contains many health-giving properties – and there are phytoestrogens present in both the fennel and the parsley.

About 2 pounds fresh sardines, scaled and gutted
½ cup pine nuts
Lemon wedges, to serve

For the marinade
⅔ cup olive oil
Juice of 1 lemon
Juice of 1 small orange

2–3 garlic cloves, crushed
½ fennel bulb, cut into matchstick strips, any feathery fronds reserved for garnishing
2 tablespoons chopped parsley, plus more whole sprigs for garnishing
Freshly ground sea salt and black pepper

Serves 4

At least an hour ahead, make the marinade by mixing all the ingredients and seasoning well. Transfer to a shallow bowl and add the sardines. Leave to marinate in a cool place, turning from time to time. Preheat a hot broiler or barbecue, or a griddle pan.

Shaking as much of the marinade off as you can and, reserving it, broil the sardines for about five to eight minutes on each side, depending on size, until well colored and cooked through.

While they are cooking, put the marinade in a small pan and bring to a simmer. Simmer for four to five minutes, until the fennel is just tender. At the same time, roast the pine nuts in a dry skillet until lightly browned and aromatic.

Serve the broiled sardines with the marinade spooned over them and the pine nuts sprinkled on top of that. Garnish with any reserved fennel fronds and parsley sprigs, and serve with lemon wedges. Nutty mash (see page 98) makes an excellent accompaniment to these beautifully aromatic sardines.

P ** E **** A *
PHYTOESTROGENS COME IN THE FORM OF THE FENNEL AND THE PARSLEY. THE SARDINES AND PINE NUTS SUPPLY BOTH OMEGA 3 AND OMEGA 6 EFAS.

herring with oatmeal

Herrings are a very underrated fish, full of flavor, but also rich in Omega 3 oils. The oatmeal is not only a phytoestrogen but also a good source of fiber, and the oat bran (in the oats) is also beneficial for the heart. Herrings in oatmeal is a traditional Scottish dish and it is great served with Braised Red Cabbage (see page 110).

4 boned herrings
1 egg
Freshly ground sea salt and black pepper
About 1 cup fine oatmeal or rolled oats
2 tablespoons olive oil
About 1 tablespoon butter
1 tablespoon chopped parsley, for garnishing
Lemon wedges, for serving

Serves 4

If you can't get your fishmonger to bone the herring for you then cut off the heads of the fish and gut them, cutting them open from head to tail. Run your thumbs down the back to detach the spines, then ease these away from the skin and flesh. Use some tweezers to pull out as many of the remaining bones as possible.

In a large shallow bowl, beat the egg with some salt and pepper. Put the oatmeal in another bowl and season that.

Heat the oil and butter in a large skillet. Dip each flattened fish first in the egg, making sure it is coated well, and then in the oatmeal, pressing firmly. Fry over medium heat for about six minutes on each side. You'll probably have to do this in batches, so layer the cooked herrings on paper towels and keep warm in a low oven while you cook the rest.

Serve garnished with parsley and lemon wedges.

P ** E **** A *
THE OATMEAL SUPPLIES PHYTOESTROGENS AND HERRINGS ARE AN EXCELLENT SOURCE OF ESSENTIAL FATTY ACIDS.

4

main courses

vegetable yogurt moussaka

Made with added nuts and dried fruit, this moussaka is the perfect thing for casual entertaining, and if you use all or part wild mushrooms, you have quite a sophisticated dish. The moussaka contains phytoestrogens in the form of the soy flour, soy yogurt, soy milk, and mushrooms. The almonds give good amounts of essential fatty acids, and antioxidants are provided by the tomatoes, apricots, and zucchini – which are also an excellent source of beta-carotene, vitamin C, and folic acid. I have always suspected there was a better way of preparing eggplant than all that business with salting and then frying them in, ultimately, gallons of oil. This method of first baking them in a spicy coating produces a much lighter and tastier result.

About 4 tablespoons olive oil, plus more for greasing
1 tablespoon ground cumin
1 tablespoon ground ginger
1 tablespoon ground cinnamon
2 teaspoons freshly grated nutmeg
¾ cup soy flour
Freshly ground sea salt and black pepper
⅓–½ cup soy milk
2 pounds large eggplant, thinly sliced
2 recipe quantities Basic Tomato Sauce (see page 152)
1 pound zucchini, sliced
8 ounces chestnut mushrooms, sliced (about 2 cups)
2 tablespoons butter
½ cup split almonds, lightly toasted (optional)
½ cup dried apricots, chopped (optional)
3 ounces seedless raisins – about ¾ cup (optional)
2 eggs, lightly beaten
1¾ cups plain runny yogurt, ideally soy yogurt
2 tablespoons lemon juice
2 tablespoons fresh mint, chopped
1 cup Parmesan cheese, freshly grated

Serves 6–8

Preheat the oven to 375°F and oil a baking sheet and a large ovenproof casserole.

In a shallow bowl, mix half the spices with the flour and one teaspoon each of salt and pepper. Put the milk in another shallow bowl. One by one, dip the eggplant slices in the soy milk and then in the seasoned flour, shaking off any excess, and arrange on a baking sheet. Bake for 25 minutes only.

While they are baking, make the tomato sauce, adding the remaining spices to the tomatoes. In separate pans or one after the other, lightly sauté the zucchini and mushrooms in the butter with the oil until just softened. Season to taste and set aside in a warm place.

When the eggplant slices are ready, remove them from the oven and reduce the setting to 350°F. Put a layer of one-quarter of the eggplant in the bottom of the casserole. If you are using them, mix the almonds and dried fruit into the tomato sauce when it is ready.

Spoon one-third of the sauce over the eggplant layer, followed by the mushrooms, followed by another layer of sauce, a layer of zucchini, a final layer of tomato sauce, and a final top layer of eggplant.

In a bowl, mix the eggs into the yogurt, followed by the lemon juice and mint. Pour over the dish. Sprinkle the Parmesan over the top and bake for 45 minutes, until uniformly golden brown.

P **** E ** A ****
THERE ARE PHYTOESTROGENS IN THE SOY FLOUR, SOY YOGURT, SOY MILK, AND MUSHROOMS, AND ANTIOXIDANTS IN THE FRUIT AND VEGETABLES.

vegetable tempura

This dish contains some wonderful, healthy ingredients, but should be kept for special occasions: frying oil at high temperatures can mean that the oil is damaged through the high temperature and creates free radicals. It is fine to treat yourself occasionally though, and the vinegar in the dipping sauce helps to break down the oils.

3 zucchini
1 large eggplant
1 head of broccoli
6 ounces large
   Portobello mushrooms
8 ounces asparagus (about
   8–10 spears)
3 ounces sesame seeds
Olive oil for deep-frying
For the dipping sauce
⅓–½ cup miso broth
   (see page 150) or vegetable
   broth (see page 151)
2 tablespoons soy sauce
2 tablespoons cider vinegar
2 tablespoons mirin (Japanese
   rice wine)

Freshly ground sea salt and
   black pepper

For the tempura batter
1 large egg, plus 1 extra yolk
1½ cups ice water
1½ cups all-purpose flour, plus
   more for coating
1½ teaspoons baking powder
1 teaspoon salt

To serve
Fresh ginger root or Japanese
   pickled ginger, grated
Daikon (Japanese radish) or
   wasabi, freshly grated
Soy sauce

Serves 6

First make the dipping sauce: mix all the ingredients together in a small pan and place over a low heat to warm through.

Prepare the vegetables: slice the zucchini and eggplant across at an angle to give interestingly shaped slices. Separate the broccoli into bite-sized florets. Cut the mushrooms across into thickish slices. Tim the asparagus and cut in half if big. Pat all the vegetables thoroughly dry with paper towels.

When you are ready to fry, make the tempura batter: in a large bowl, beat the egg and extra yolk until just mixed. Stir in the iced water, then sift over the flour, baking powder, and salt.

Stir until just combined – do not over-mix (there should still be visible flecks of flour) or the batter will be heavy.

Preheat a low oven to 375°F and heat the oil for deep-frying very hot, so that a stale bread cube will brown in it in 40 seconds.

To cook the vegetables, toss the pieces one at a time in flour and then dip them in the batter to coat completely, shake off any excess and sprinkle with sesame seeds. Drop them into the hot oil for two to three minutes, until golden, then remove with a slotted spoon, and drain on paper towels. You will probably have to work in batches (never overcrowd the pan when deep-frying as this lowers the cooking temperature too much and the batter or food goes soggy): keep the cooked pieces hot in the warm oven with the door open until all are cooked. Serve hot with the dipping sauce and accompaniments.

P ** (WITH ADDED TOFU ****) E * A **
PHYTOESTROGENS FROM THE MISO BROTH AND BROCCOLI, INCREASED BY USING TOFU AS WELL AS VEGETABLES. ESSENTIAL FATTY ACIDS IN THE SESAME SEEDS.

frittedda palermitana

A traditional Sicilian artichoke, pea, and lima bean stew. Artichokes contain cynarin, a substance which improves liver function and has been said to stimulate liver cell regeneration. The liver must function optimally at menopause so that the "bad" estrogens are converted into "good" ones.

6 large globe artichokes or
   12–15 small young artichokes
Juice of ½ lemon
¾ cup olive oil
10½ ounces large whole shallots
1 pound shelled peas
1 pound shelled fresh lima beans

Freshly ground sea salt and
   black pepper
⅓–½ cup dry white wine
2 tablespoons chopped flat-
   leaf parsley, plus more whole
   leaves for garnishing
Croûtes of good crusty bread
   fried in olive oil, to serve
   (optional)

Serves 6

First prepare the artichokes. For large artichokes, cut off the stalk and cut across to remove the top third of the leaves, remove any coarse outer leaves and cut in half lengthwise to remove the hairy choke inside, then cut each half again lengthwise into three pieces. Young artichokes (which have not developed their chokes) need only be trimmed of tough stalks and coarse outer leaves, then quartered. As they are prepared, drop them into a bowl of water mixed with with the lemon juice to prevent discoloration.

Heat the oil in a large heavy-bottomed saucepan and fry the shallots gently until soft and translucent. Add the artichokes, peas, and lima beans with seasoning to taste, followed by the wine and a ladleful of water and bring to a boil. Lower the heat to a gentle simmer, cover tightly, and cook gently for about 20 minutes, or until the vegetables are tender. Stir from time to time and add a little more water if at any time it looks too dry. Add the chopped parsley for the last five minutes of cooking.

Serve hot, with croûtes of crusty bread fried in olive oil if you like, garnished with more whole parsley leaves.

P ** E * A *
PHYTOESTROGENS ARE PROVIDED BY THE PARSLEY, BEANS, AND PEAS.

vegetable, bean-sprout, and tofu stir-fry

Stir-fries are easy to make and very good for you; the nutrients from the vegetables are not lost through heavy cooking. A mix of phytoestrogens is provided by the tofu, broccoli, mushroom, and bean sprouts. There is also a plentiful supply of anti-aging and anti-cancer antioxidants.

About 2 tablespoons olive oil
6 scallions, cut across at an
   angle into 1-inch lengths
1–2 red chiles, seeded and
   finely chopped
10 ounces tofu, cut into small
   bite-sized cubes
2 sweet peppers (preferably red
   and yellow), seeded and cut
   into strips
3½ ounces snow peas

3½ ounces baby corn,
   cut in half
3½ ounces broccoli, separated
   into bite-sized pieces
2 cups (roughly 8 or 9) cherry
   tomatoes
3½ ounces chestnut
   mushrooms, halved
3½ ounces bok choy, choy sum
   or other Chinese leaves, torn
   into large pieces (about 1 cup)
7 ounces bean sprouts
Soy sauce to taste
Small splash of sesame oil

Serves 4

Heat the oil in a large wok until quite hot and then add the scallion and chiles. Stir-fry until wilted and aromatic; two to three minutes. Remove with a slotted spoon and keep warm in a bowl.

Add the tofu and stir-fry until well colored. Again remove from the wok with a slotted spoon and keep warm in the bowl.

Add the peppers, peas, corn, and broccoli and stir-fry for two to three minutes, then add the tomatoes and mushrooms and stir-fry for two more minutes. Remove and keep warm in the bowl.

Add the Chinese leaves to the wok and stir-fry until wilted. Now return all the other items from the bowl to the wok, together with the bean sprouts. Turn over medium heat for a minute or so, seasoning to taste with the soy sauce and sesame oil, until all is well warmed through. Serve at once.

P ***** E * A ***
PHYTOS IN THE TOFU, BROCCOLI, MUSHROOM, AND BEAN SPROUTS. ANTIOXIDANTS IN THE PEPPERS, SNOW PEAS, CORN, BROCCOLI, AND TOMATOES.

wild mushroom risotto

The wonderfully versatile mushroom, which transforms so many dishes, is a classic risotto ingredient. You could use either miso broth or vegetable broth, but the miso is a good source of phytoestrogens. The shallots and garlic are from the allium family, which is known to boost the immune system and have anti-cancer qualities.

2 ounces dried cèpes
6¼ cups miso broth (see page 150) or vegetable stock
  (see page 151)
½ stick butter
4 tablespoons olive oil
6 shallots, finely chopped
3 garlic cloves, crushed
2 cups arborio rice
⅓–½ cup red wine (optional)
About 12 ounces mixed fresh wild mushrooms (such as cèpes,
  chanterelles, blewitts, and trompettes de mort)
Freshly ground sea salt and black pepper
3 tablespoons parsley, chopped
1½ cups Parmesan cheese, freshly grated

Serves 4-6

Rinse the cèpes, put them in a small heatproof bowl and cover them with boiling water. Leave to rehydrate for about 20 minutes, drain, reserving the liquid, and chop quite finely.

Put the broth in a saucepan and bring it to just below a boil. Keep it there throughout the operation.

Heat one-third of the butter and half the oil in a large heavy-bottomed saucepan. Add the shallots and sauté until just translucent, then add the cèpes and the garlic cloves and sauté for another three to four minutes.

Add the rice and stir around for a couple of minutes to coat well. Add the wine (if using) and boil it off (the saucepan gets really hot when you are stirring in the rice), then add the liquid from soaking the cèpes and stir until it is absorbed.

Add a large ladleful of broth and stir until all the liquid is absorbed. Continue to add broth in the same way, for about 15–20 minutes, until the rice is tender but still firm to the bite and the risotto creamy and moist (if you run out of broth before the rice is tender, just add ladlefuls of boiling water).

Towards the end of this process, heat half the remaining butter and all the remaining oil in a large skillet and cook each variety of mushroom separately, frying them until they just color on each side. Transfer them to a warmed bowl as they are cooked. Season the cooked mushrooms really well and stir in the parsley.

When the risotto is ready, beat the remaining butter and the cheese into it. Stir in the mushrooms and adjust the seasoning if necessary. Cover and leave to stand for about five minutes before serving.

P *** E * A **
GOOD LEVELS OF PHYTOESTROGENS IN THE MUSHROOMS, FURTHERED BY THE PLANT HORMONES IN THE MISO BROTH, RICE, AND PARSLEY.

mixed vegetable stew with herb dumplings

Stew is always a real comfort on cold days, and so rich in flavor. This warming dish has plenty of powerful antioxidants: beta-carotene in the carrots and lycopene in the tomatoes. If chile tends to bring on hot flashes in you, omit it.

2 tablespoons olive oil
4 medium onions, chopped
3–4 garlic cloves, finely chopped
2–3 small hot red chiles, seeded and finely chopped (optional)
8 ounces carrots, thickly sliced at an angle
8 ounces potatoes, cut into bite-sized cubes
8 ounces leeks, thickly sliced at an angle
1/3–1/2 cup red wine (optional)
14 ounces canned chopped plum tomatoes
1¼ cups miso broth (see page 150) or vegetable stock
   (see page 151)
1 bouquet garni
1 tablespoon fennel seeds
1 tablespoon celery seeds
2 tablespoons sesame seeds
Freshly ground sea salt and black pepper
6 ounces shelled or frozen peas (about 1½ cups)
6 ounces green beans
8 ounces zucchini, thickly sliced at an angle

For the herb dumplings
3 sticks cold butter, shredded in a grater
2/3 cup self-rising flour, plus more for dusting
1 tablespoon soy flour
Freshly ground sea salt and black pepper
About 6 tablespoons finely chopped mixed fresh herbs such as
   parsley, chives, thyme, and basil
About 5 tablespoons soy milk

Serves 6–8

Heat the oil in a large flameproof casserole and, when hot, sauté the onions until just translucent. Add the garlic and chiles, and sauté for a minute or two more. Add the carrots, potatoes, and leeks and toss to coat. Add the wine (if using) and boil to reduce it to a sticky residue.

Next add the tomatoes with their liquid, the broth, bouquet garni, and the seeds. Season well and bring to a boil. Reduce the heat, cover, and simmer gently (or cook in the oven at 300°F) for about 45 minutes.

Towards the end of that time, prepare the dumplings: in a mixing bowl, rub the butter roughly into the sifted flours with seasoning to taste, until the mixture resembles coarse crumbs. Stir in the herbs and add just enough of the milk to mix to a soft dough. Using floured hands, form the dough into about 18–20 small balls.

After the 45 minutes, take the casserole out of the oven (if it is in there) or remove from the heat. Remove the bouquet garni and discard it. Favoring the potatoes above all, carefully transfer about one-quarter of the casserole's contents to a food processor, and puree until fairly smooth, but not too smooth.

Pour the pureed mixture back into the casserole and stir in the remaining vegetables, then float the dumplings on top. Bring back to a simmer on the stove, cover again, and then either continue to simmer or return to the oven for a further 20 minutes.

P **** E ** A ****
PHYTOESTROGENS ARE SUPPLIED BY THE MISO BROTH, SEEDS, SOY MILK, AND SOY FLOUR. POWERFUL ANTIOXIDANTS VIA THE CARROTS AND TOMATOES.

vegetable masala

As well as making a nice change for a weekday meal, this also makes an unusual accompaniment to roast, baked, or broiled fish for a weekend lunch. The vegetables offer a good supply of antioxidants and the miso broth, potatoes, carrots, and broccoli are rich in phytoestrogens.

2 medium potatoes
Sea salt and black pepper
2 teaspoons coriander seeds
1 teaspoon fennel seeds
1 teaspoon cumin seeds
3 tablespoons olive oil
2 large onions, chopped
3–4 garlic cloves, finely chopped
2–3 hot red chiles, seeded and finely chopped
½-inch piece of ginger root, finely chopped
8 ounces carrots, sliced
½ cauliflower, chopped

6 ounces broccoli, separated into bite-sized florets and stalks cut into cubes
6 ounces green beans
14 ounces canned chopped plum tomatoes
2 tablespoons tomato paste
1 tablespoon honey
1¼ cups miso broth (see page 150) or vegetable stock (see page 151)
2 teaspoons garam masala
2 tablespoons chopped cilantro, plus more whole sprigs for garnishing

Serves 4–6 as a main course

Parboil the potatoes for about 10 minutes in plenty of boiling salted water. Drain, and when cool, cut into bite-sized cubes.

Lightly crush all the spices and seeds using a pestle and mortar. Heat two tablespoons of oil in a large heavy-bottomed pot, then sauté the spices on a fairly high heat until sizzling. Add the onions, sauté until they are just translucent, then add the garlic, chiles, and ginger, and sauté for a minute or two more.

Add all the fresh vegetables and shake over medium heat for a few minutes to coat them well in the oil and spices. Add the tomatoes with their liquid, the tomato paste, honey, and broth, and season to taste. Stir well, cover and cook gently for about 15–20 minutes, until the vegetables are just tender.

Heat the remaining oil and cook the garam masala for one or two minutes. Stir into the vegetables, add the cilantro and cook for two to three minutes. Garnish with cilantro sprigs.

P *** E * A ***

lentil and fruit pilaf

Lentils are a wonderful source of phytoestrogens because they contain all four isoflavones. Further plant hormones are found in the rice, cinnamon, parsley, and soy yogurt. The almonds are a good source of essential oils, but use them only lightly toasted or raw to avoid destroying the nutrients.

6 ounces green lentils (about ¾ cup)
Freshly ground sea salt and black pepper
2¼ cups basmati rice
¼ cup seedless raisins
2–3 pitted dates, chopped
2–3 dried figs, chopped
1 tablespoon rose water or orange flower water

1 teaspoon ground cinnamon
2 tablespoons chopped flat-leaf parsley, plus more whole sprigs for garnishing
¾ cup split blanched almonds, lightly toasted in a dry skillet
3 tablespoons extra virgin olive oil
Yogurt, preferably soy yogurt, for serving

Serves 4

Rinse the lentils well and put them in a large saucepan of fresh water. Bring to a boil and boil for 20–30 minutes until just tender, adding salt only after the lentils start to soften (otherwise the skins toughen). Drain well.

While the lentils are cooking, rinse the rice well under running cold water, drain, and then put into a saucepan of boiling salted water. Bring back to the boil, stir well, lower the heat and simmer until just tender, 8–10 minutes. Drain well.

Mix the dried fruit, rose water, or orange flower water and cinnamon in a bowl.

In a large heavy-bottomed saucepan, arrange layers of rice, lentils, and dried fruit, seasoning each layer and sprinkling some parsley and almonds over the top (reserving some of each for garnish). Drizzle over the olive oil, cover, and cook very gently for 15–20 minutes.

Serve garnished with some parsley sprigs and accompanied by a bowl of yogurt.

P ***** E ** A **
PHYTOESTROGENS VIA THE LENTILS, RICE, CINNAMON, PARSLEY, AND SOY YOGURT. THE DRIED FRUITS ARE RICH IN ANTIOXIDANTS.

masoor dhal with cabbage

Lentils supply all four isoflavones and so are an excellent source of plant hormones. The cabbage, gives good anti-cancer protection by helping estrogen to be excreted in its harmless form. Serve with basmati rice or Cinnamon Rice (see page 121).

8 ounces masoor dhal (red split lentils), well rinsed
Good pinch of ground turmeric
3 tablespoons olive oil
1 teaspoon cumin seeds
3 garlic cloves, finely chopped
1 large onion, thinly sliced
1 hot red chile, seeded and finely chopped (optional), plus more sliced chiles for garnishing

8 ounces firm cabbage, finely shredded
Freshly ground sea salt and black pepper
½ teaspoon finely grated ginger root
14 ounces canned chopped plum tomatoes
½ teaspoon garam masala
1 tablespoon finely chopped cilantro leaves, plus more whole leaves for garnishing

Serves 4

Put the lentils in a large heavy saucepan, add 3¾ cups of fresh water, and bring to a boil. Skim off any scum and stir in the turmeric. Turn down the heat, partially cover, and leave to simmer gently, stirring from time to time.

While the lentils are cooking, heat the oil in a large skillet over medium heat. Add the cumin seeds and sauté for a few seconds. Add the garlic and toss until just beginning to color, then add the onion, chile, and cabbage. Stir-fry for a few minutes until the cabbage begins to color and become crisp. Season and set aside.

When the lentils have been cooking for 1¼ hours, stir in the ginger, tomatoes, and garam masala, and season to taste. Cook over medium heat, partially covered, for 10 minutes more. Add the contents of the pan together with the cilantro to the lentils, heat gently and serve, garnished with whole cilantro and sliced chile.

P ***** E * A ***
PHYTOESTROGENS FROM THE LENTILS AND RICE. THE POWERFUL ANTIOXIDANT, LYCOPENE, COMES FROM THE TOMATOES.

boston baked beans

You need a variety of legumes to supply your phytoestrogen needs. They are contained in the haricot or navy beans. The seaweed flakes provide iodine, vital for healthy thyroid function and its anti-cancer benefits. Antioxidants are found in the tomato ketchup and red wine.

2⅓ cups dried haricot beans, preferably navy beans, rinsed and soaked overnight
2 tablespoons butter
2 tablespoons olive oil
3 large onions, chopped
4 garlic cloves, finely chopped
1 ounce mixed dried seaweed flakes
2½ cups Tomato Ketchup (see page 152)

4 tablespoons maple syrup
4 tablespoons dark molasses
3 tablespoons no-added-sugar Worcestershire sauce
3 tablespoons red wine
1 tablespoon cider vinegar
2 teaspoons mustard powder
Freshly ground sea salt and black pepper
Chopped parsley, for garnishing (optional)
Bread or toast, preferably whole-wheat, for serving

Serves 6 (with second helpings!)

Drain the beans, rinse well again and put in a large heavy saucepan. Cover generously with fresh (unsalted) water and bring to a boil. Reduce the heat, and simmer gently until just tender, 50–90 minutes, depending on the beans. When cooked, drain the beans, reserving the cooking water.

Preheat the oven to 300°F. Heat the butter and oil in a large flameproof casserole over medium heat and sauté the onions and garlic until translucent.

Stir the seaweed, tomato ketchup, syrup, molasses, Worcestershire sauce, wine, cider vinegar, and mustard into three-quarter cup of the reserved bean cooking liquid. Stir this into the casserole, simmer, and mix in the beans. Season. Cover and cook in the oven for two to three hours, scraping up the bottom layer from time to time to prevent burning and adding a little water if at any time it seems too dry. Uncover the casserole for the last 30 minutes or so to brown the top. Serve immediately, served on toast or accompanied by good bread and garnished with some chopped parsley, if you like.

P **** E * A *

mixed bean and tomato casserole

Another warming and nourishing dish, this stew gives plenty of phytoestrogens from the different mix of beans, and the miso broth. The seaweed flakes provide vital trace minerals, and the tomatoes the antioxidant lycopene. Try the stew with a crisp green salad.

2 tablespoons olive oil
2 large onions, chopped
2–3 garlic cloves, finely chopped
1–2 small hot red chiles, seeded and finely chopped (optional)
⅓–½ cup red wine (optional)
Two 14-ounce cans of chopped plum tomatoes
5 tablespoons tomato paste
1¼ cups miso broth (see page 150) or vegetable stock (see page 151)
Large handful of mixed dried seaweed flakes
2 teaspoons dried thyme

2 teaspoons dried oregano
1 teaspoon dried sage
2 tablespoons flat-leaf parsley, chopped
Freshly ground sea salt and black pepper
14 ounces canned butter beans, drained
14 ounces canned or bottled cannellini beans, drained
14 ounces canned red kidney beans, drained

For the topping
½ cup whole-wheat bread crumbs
1 ounce peanuts, crushed
1 tablespoon butter, melted

Serves 4

Preheat the oven to 350°F.

Heat the oil in a large flameproof casserole and, when hot, sauté the onions until just translucent. Add the garlic and chiles (if using) and sauté for a minute or two more. Add the wine (if using) and boil to reduce to a sticky residue. Then add the tomatoes with their liquid, the tomato paste, broth, seaweed flakes, and the dried and fresh herbs. Season to taste, mix well, and simmer for about 15 minutes.

Spread a quarter of the mixture in the bottom of an ovenproof casserole, then layer up the beans, with a layer of tomato mixture between them. Finish with a layer of tomato mixture.

Mix the topping ingredients and sprinkle evenly over the stew. Bake for 30 minutes, until the topping is browned.

P ***** E ** A ***

hoppin' john with greens

This dish is said to bring good fortune if eaten on New Year's Day. Served with salad, it makes good eating any day of the year. For more nutrients, cook the beans with kombu (seaweed), as mentioned in Shopping and Cooking Tips (see page 42).

1⅓ cups black-eyed peas
1 large onion, chopped
2 garlic cloves, finely chopped
Pinch of dried red pepper flakes
1 bay leaf
2 large handfuls of mixed
　seaweed flakes

Freshly ground sea salt and
　black pepper
8 ounces collard greens,
　spring greens or kale,
　shredded
2 cups long-grain brown rice
2 tablespoons butter
Cayenne pepper

Serves 4–6

Cover the black-eyed peas in cold water and soak overnight. Next day, drain and rinse them, then measure them by volume in a measuring jug. Put them in a large pan with three-and-a-half times their volume of fresh cold water. Bring to a boil and boil hard for five minutes, then leave to stand for an hour.

Add the onion, garlic, red pepper flakes, bay leaf, half the seaweed flakes, and black pepper to taste. Bring to a boil again, lower the heat, cover, and simmer for another one to one-and-a-half hours, until the beans are tender. Towards the end of the cooking time, cook the greens in a separate saucepan of salted water with the remaining seaweed flakes until just tender, drain well, and keep warm.

At the same time, cook the long-grain rice in a separate saucepan of salted water until just tender but still al dente. Drain well, and then fluff over very low heat.

When the beans are cooked, mash some of them a little with a fork, then stir in the greens, rice, and butter. This gives a mixed consistency. Adjust the seasoning to taste with pepper, salt, and cayenne, and heat through gently before serving.

P **** E * A ***
THE BLACK-EYED PEAS ARE HIGH IN PHYTOESTROGENS. THE DARK GREEN LEAFY VEGETABLES OFFER EXCELLENT QUANTITIES OF ANTIOXIDANTS.

tofu and mushroom stroganoff

Stroganoff is a lovely way to vary the taste of tofu by marinating it so it can pick up all the different flavors. The rice or noodles will supply additional phytoestrogens to those in the tofu and the mushrooms, and the onions are believed to help prevent bones from thinning.

1 tablespoon dark soy sauce
1 tablespoon no-added-sugar
　Worcestershire sauce
2 tablespoons sweet paprika
Freshly ground sea salt and
　black pepper
8 ounces soft tofu, cut into
　bite-sized strips
3 tablespoons olive oil

2 large onions, cut in half and
　sliced
1 tablespoon butter
4 cups chestnut mushrooms,
　sliced
1¼ cups sour cream or crème
　fraîche
Lemon juice to taste
Boiled basmati rice or fresh egg
　noodles, for serving

Serves 4–6

Well ahead of time, mix the soy and Worcestershire sauces with half the paprika and some seasoning in a shallow bowl. Toss the tofu strips in the mixture and leave to marinate for at least 30 minutes, stirring from time to time.

Heat two tablespoons of the oil in a large skillet and sauté the onions with the paprika until the onions are translucent.

Add the marinated tofu with any liquid left in the bowl and continue to sauté until the tofu is well browned all over and the onions lightly browned. Transfer the contents of the saucepan to a bowl and keep warm.

Heat the remaining oil in the pan with the butter and sauté the chestnut mushrooms until well colored. Add the contents of the bowl back to the pan, together with the sour cream or crème fraîche. Mix well, season to taste with salt, pepper, and lemon juice, and bring back to a simmer for a minute or two.

Serve with rice or noodles.

P **** E * A *
THE RICE, NOODLES, TOFU, AND MUSHROOMS WILL ALL SUPPLY GOOD AMOUNTS OF PHYTOESTROGENS.

vegetable chili

Chili is an ever-popular family meal. It includes phytoestrogens from the kidney beans, miso broth, and carrots, and excellent helpings of antioxidants from the carrots, zucchini, and tomatoes. Essential nutrients are supplied by the seaweed flakes, including iodine for a healthy working thyroid. If hot food tends to bring on hot flashes, omit the chiles.

4 tablespoons olive oil
1 teaspoon ground cumin
1 teaspoon ground cinnamon
1 teaspoon fennel seeds
2 teaspoons sesame seeds
1 teaspoon dried oregano
Chili powder to taste (optional)
2 onions, chopped
2 garlic cloves, finely chopped
2 peppers, preferably of different colors, seeded and
    cut into thick strips
2 hot red chiles, seeded (if you don't want the dish too hot)
    and finely chopped
4 tablespoons red wine (optional)
3–4 carrots, cut into strips
3–4 zucchini, cut into strips
14 ounces canned chopped plum tomatoes
3 tablespoons tomato paste
About 3¾ cups miso broth (see page 150) or fish
    or seafood broth (see page 151)
2 large cans of red kidney beans, drained
Handful of mixed seaweed flakes
Freshly ground sea salt and black pepper
3 tablespoons chopped cilantro, plus more sprigs for garnishing
Juice of 1 lemon

To serve
Sour cream
Red onion, chopped
Mature Cheddar cheese, grated

Serves 4–6

Heat the oil in a large and deep heavy-bottomed saucepan. When hot, cook all the spices, seeds, and oregano in the oil for a minute or two over medium heat, until aromatic. Then lower the heat and sauté the onion until translucent. Add the garlic, pepper strips, and chiles, and sauté briefly until just beginning to soften. Add the red wine (if using) and cook, uncovered, until reduced right down.

At the same time, in a separate saucepan sauté the carrot batons in the remaining oil for about five minutes. Then add the zucchini and sauté together for about five minutes more, until both vegetables are just softened.

When the wine has reduced, add the tomatoes, tomato paste, and broth to the saucepan with the beans, sautéed vegetables, and seaweed. Season to taste and bring to a boil. Lower the heat, cover, and simmer gently for about 30 minutes.

Stir in the cilantro and lemon juice and cook for 10 minutes more. Serve with separate bowls of sour cream, chopped red onion, and grated Cheddar.

Variation: if you want to boost the dish's phyto content, stir a spoonful or two of linseeds into the chili just before serving, or mix into the sour cream.

P **** E *** A ****
PHYTOESTROGENS FROM THE KIDNEY BEANS, MISO BROTH, AND CARROTS; ANTIOXIDANTS FROM THE CARROTS, ZUCCHINI, AND TOMATOES..

herby tofu and oat sausages with nutty mash

There is such a variety of goodness in this one delicious dish. The oatmeal is especially good for maintaining healthy cholesterol levels as well as supplying excellent levels of fiber, which helps to prevent unwanted "old" estrogens circulating in the body.

2⅓ cups oatmeal, plus more for coating
9 ounces silken tofu
Handful of fresh thyme
Large bunch of fresh chives
Large handful of flat-leaf parsley
Large handful of mixed dried seaweed flakes
3 tablespoons hummus (see page 71 or preservative-free ready-made)
2 cups mature Cheddar cheese, coarsely grated
1 tablespoon honey
2 tablespoons soy sauce
1 tablespoon no-added-sugar Worcestershire sauce

1 egg
Freshly ground sea salt and black pepper
Flour, for dusting
Olive oil, for frying

For the nutty mash
2¼ pounds potatoes
2 tablespoons walnut oil
2 tablespoons olive oil
Freshly ground sea salt and black pepper
½ cup almonds, finely chopped
3 tablespoons flat-leaf parsley, chopped

Makes 8–10

Put all the ingredients for the sausages in a food processor with generous seasoning to taste and process until cohering together. Do not over-mix or the sausages will be too dense.

With floured hands, form the mixture into small tennis ball-sized spheres, roll on a coating of more oats and then pat these out into sausage shapes (try to give them four long flat sides as this will make the frying easier). Chill for about 10 minutes. (If you had trouble getting good shapes, they will be easier to shape after chilling.)

While they are chilling, cook the potatoes for the mash in boiling salted water until tender. Drain well, and steam dry in the hot saucepan. Keep warm.

Fry the sausages gently in hot olive oil, turning regularly, until well browned on all sides, about 15–20 minutes in all.

Mash the dried potatoes, adding the walnut and olive oils and seasoning. Finish by mixing in the chopped nuts and parsley.

Serve at once, accompanied by the nutty mashed potatoes.

Variations: you can make a nice "gravy" for these sausages by thickening some miso broth (see page 150) with arrowroot and serving the sausages with some fried onions, into which some sesame seeds and/or linseeds have been mixed.

P ***** E ** A *
PLANT HORMONES ARE AVAILABLE FROM THE OATMEAL, TOFU, HUMMUS (MADE FROM CHICKPEAS), PARSLEY, AND POTATOES.

pasta with roast garlic and pine nuts

You don't have to roast garlic especially for this dish; next time you are roasting anything, simply pop a few extra heads in the oven. Use right away with whatever you are cooking, and keep three in the fridge for this dish. Parmesan is optional in this dish; but do offer a fresh green or tomato salad.

3 large heads of garlic
About 2 tablespoons olive oil
4 cups (preferably whole-wheat) pasta, such as tagliatelle, tagliarini, or linguine

Freshly ground sea salt and black pepper
1 tablespoon flaxseed oil
½ cup pine nuts, lightly toasted
3 tablespoons chopped flat-leaf parsley or basil, plus more whole sprigs for garnishing

Serves 4

Preheat the oven to 350°F. Leaving the heads of garlic intact, remove the papery outer skin. Brush the heads all over with olive oil and arrange in a small ovenproof dish that is just big enough to hold them in a single layer. Add a splash of water and cover with an ovenproof lid. Bake for about 30 minutes, until tender. Allow to cool until they can be handled.

Towards the end of the roasting time, start cooking the pasta in a large pan of boiling salted water, until the pasta is *al dente*, i.e., soft but still offering some resistance when you bite into it.

While the pasta is cooking, take one of the garlic heads and squeeze the softened garlic from all its cloves. Puree this with the flaxseed oil and remaining olive oil. Carefully peel the rest of the garlic cloves to keep them intact. Mix these with the garlic puree, pine nuts, parsley or basil, and seasoning.

When the pasta is ready, drain well, tip it into the sauce and toss to dress uniformly. Garnish with some parsley or basil sprigs, and serve immediately.

P ** E *** A *
PLENTY OF PHYTOESTROGENS FROM THE GARLIC, PARSLEY, AND WHOLE-WHEAT PASTA. FLAXSEED OIL AND PINE NUTS GIVE OMEGA 3 AND 6 ESSENTIAL OILS.

deluxe kabobs

These kabobs are a great way to serve tofu. Shrimp are a rich source of selenium and sesame seeds contain phytoestrogens and essential fatty acids as well.

6 red onions, quartered
7 ounces firm tofu, cut into large bite-sized pieces
18 raw giant shrimp, shelled and de-veined but with tails
6 large vine-ripened tomatoes, quartered
3 large peppers, preferably of different colors, quartered and seeded
6 large Portobello mushrooms, cut into thick slices
12 bay leaves
Sea salt and black pepper
2½ tablespoons sesame seeds
Lemon wedges, for serving

For the marinade
6 tablespoons olive oil
1 tablespoon soy sauce
2 tablespoons honey
1½-inch piece of ginger root, crushed
3 garlic cloves, crushed
2 tablespoons mirin (Japanese rice wine)
3 tablespoons oregano, chopped
1–2 red chiles, seeded and finely chopped
Freshly ground sea salt and black pepper

Serves 6

Several hours ahead: mix all the marinade ingredients, except one-third of the oregano, in a large shallow bowl with seasoning to taste. Toss the red onions, tofu, and shrimp in the mixture. Cover and marinate in the fridge for at least three hours.

Preheat a hot broiler or light a barbecue. Drain the onions, tofu, and shrimp from the marinade and thread them on six skewers interleaved with pieces of tomato, pepper, mushroom, and bay leaves. Season if necessary and sprinkle with sesame seeds. Grill until browned on all sides, occasionally basting with the marinade. Garnish with lemon wedges and reserved oregano.

Variation: for an Indonesian satay effect you could use Peanut Sauce as the marinade (see page 155).

P **** E ** A ****
PHYTOESTROGENS FROM THE TOFU AND SESAME SEEDS, EFAS FROM THE SHRIMP AND SESAME SEEDS, ANTIOXIDANTS IN THE PEPPERS AND TOMATOES.

pizza marinara

Not your average pizza! Eating raw onions has been found to reduce cholesterol by increasing the "good" (HDL) cholesterol. Both raw and cooked onions can help to prevent blood clots, and so defend against heart attacks and strokes. The seaweed provides a store of vital trace minerals.

For the dough
1⅓ cups water, warmed to blood temperature
1 teaspoon honey
¾ ounce fresh yeast, or 1 sachet of easy-blend dried yeast
2 cups Italian type "00" or strong white flour, plus more for dusting
1 cup whole-wheat flour
1 cup soy flour
4 tablespoons extra virgin olive oil
Freshly ground sea salt
Good handful of mixed seaweed flakes

For the topping
12 ounces passata or canned plum tomatoes, pureed
Freshly ground sea salt and black pepper

Soy sauce
Balsamic vinegar
1 small bulb of fennel, cored and cut into bite-sized pieces
1 small red onion, halved and sliced
1 fresh (preferably buffalo) Mozzarella cheese, about 3½ ounces, cut into slices
Half a 3½-ounce can of mussels, drained
3 ounces frozen cooked and peeled large shrimp
Half a 3½-ounce can of tuna in oil, drained and separated into small bite-sized pieces
Juice of ½ lemon
A few sprigs of basil
Handful of pitted black olives
5 quail eggs (optional)
½ cup pine nuts

Serves 4–6 (makes one 12-in diameter round pizza)

To make the yeast: put 3 tablespoons of the water and the honey in a large bowl and stir in the fresh yeast (if using easy-blend yeast, add it to the flour). Mix the dough to a cream. Add 4 tablespoons of the flour and mix to a soft dough (add more flour or water if necessary). Knead for 3 minutes, sprinkle with more flour, then cover with a dish towel and let rise for 30 minutes.

Once risen, rewarm the remaining water to room temperature. Sift the remaining flours into the bowl, pour over some water and pinch the dough, flour, and water together to mix.

Gradually add more water, pinching together, until all the water is added, then repeat with one tablespoon of oil. When you have a softish ball of dough, make a dent in the top and add some salt, the seaweed flakes, and another tablespoon of oil. Knead everything together until it is no longer sticky and the inside surface of the bowl is clean. Toss the dough and stretch it into a flat shape on a floured work surface. Drizzle on one more spoonful of oil and knead, then repeat, kneading for a good minute more. The dough is ready when it feels silky, but not too silky. Put the dough back in the bowl and cut a big cross in the top with a knife. Sprinkle with flour, cover with a dish towel and leave in a warm place to double in size, about two hours.

Preheat the oven to 475°F or to its highest setting. Lightly flour the work surface again, knead or roll the risen dough on it for a few minutes, then roll it out to a round big enough to line a 12-inch diameter round pizza pan (or a large baking sheet). Press evenly into the pan, so it is slightly thinner in the middle, and leave it indented with your fingertips. Trim the edges, if necessary, and prick all over with a fork.

For the topping: season the tomato passata or puree and add a dash of soy sauce and balsamic vinegar. Spread all over the pizza base. Scatter the fennel and onion over, then add the cheese slices. Dot the mussels, shrimp, and tuna about. Sprinkle the seafood with lemon juice and the cheese with a dash of balsamic vinegar. Put some sprigs of basil on top of each cheese slice and scatter the olives. If using, break the eggs into little recesses. Finally, season well and scatter with the pine nuts.

Bake immediately for 18–20 minutes, until puffed and golden. Don't open the oven for the first 15 minutes. Let it rest out of the oven for about five minutes before serving.

P *** E **** A **
CONTAINS PHYTOESTROGENS IN THE FORM OF SOY FLOUR AND FENNEL. THE OILY FISH BRING THE OMEGA 3 ESSENTIAL FATTY OILS.

broiled seafood salad

Not only will this colorful salad transport you to the Mediterranean, but it will also give you a nutritional boost. Plenty of selenium, a powerful antioxidant, is delivered by the shellfish in addition to other antioxidants from the green vegetables and tomatoes. There are excellent essential oils from the fish and flaxseed oil.

8 ounces prepared small squid
8 ounces raw tiger shrimp, shelled
8 ounces medium scallops, cut
   in half across their thickness
8 ounces small new potatoes
12 quail eggs
1 large Romaine lettuce or 3
   Romaine hearts
1 head of radicchio
Small bunch of arugula
Small bunch of watercress
Several handfuls of various
   fresh herbs, such as flat-leaf
   parsley, chives, dill, chervil, and
   cilantro, plus more sprigs for
   garnishing
1 English cucumber
1 red onion, halved and sliced
1 small fennel bulb, cored and
   diced fairly small
18 cherry tomatoes, cut in half

Serves 6

⅓ cup salted capers, rinsed,
   drained and patted dry
1 cup pitted black olives
2 tablespoons golden flaxseeds
   (optional)

For the marinade
1 tablespoon fresh ginger root,
   finely chopped
1 garlic clove, finely chopped
2 tablespoons linseed oil
Juice of 2 limes
1 red chile, seeded and finely
   chopped (optional)
Sea salt and black pepper

For the dressing
4 tablespoons extra virgin
   olive oil
2 tablespoons walnut or flaxseed
   oil
1 tablespoon balsamic vinegar
1 tablespoon lemon juice

If necessary, remove the squid heads (with tentacles) from the tubes and rinse all the seafood well (if they've been frozen, first swish them about in large bowl of heavily salted water) and pat them dry. Remove the dark intestinal thread from the backs of the shrimp and butterfly them open so that they lie flat.

Put all the ingredients for the marinade in a bowl, season to taste, add the seafood, and toss well. Cover and chill in the refrigerator for at least one hour, stirring from time to time.

Cook the potatoes in boiling salted water until just tender. Drain and steam dry. Put another saucepan of water on to heat, add the eggs, and bring to a boil. Allow to boil for a minute only and then rinse under cold water and drain.

Next prepare the fresh vegetables: shred the lettuce and radicchio leaves into the bottom of a large salad bowl together with the arugula and watercress leaves and all but a few sprigs of each of the herbs. Slice the cucumber lengthwise into two or three long slices and then cut these into long strips, finally cut across into three-inch chunks. Add the cucumber together with the onion, fennel, and tomatoes to the bowl.

Heat a hot ridged griddle pan. Make the dressing: blend all the ingredients and season to taste. Shell the eggs and cut them in half.

Cut the potatoes into bite-sized chunks if necessary and add these to the salad with the capers, half the olives, and the linseeds if using. Pour the dressing over the salad and toss well to mix. Taste and adjust the seasoning at this stage again. Drain the seafood from the marinade and pat dry. Cook in batches on the hot griddle pan: starting with the squid, then the shrimp, and finishing with the scallops. The squid will need a minute or two on each side, as will the shrimp, while the scallops literally need only about 15 seconds on each side. Try to get some nice sear marks from the hot pan ridges on the seafood but resist the temptation to overcook (which can happen in a matter of seconds with seafood and ruin it). As they are ready, scatter them over the tops of the salad.

Arrange the egg halves over the top of the salad, together with the remaining olives and herb sprigs.

P **** E **** A *****
EFAS FROM THE FISH AND LINSEED OIL; PHYTOESTROGENS FROM THE
FLAX SEEDS AND FENNEL; ANTIOXIDANTS FROM THE SHRIMP, GREEN VEGETABLES,
AND TOMATOES.

jambalaya

This is a version of the classic rice dish from Creole cuisine served in many Louisiana homes and restaurants. It can be made with chicken, shrimp, or ham, or without meat or fish. Plant hormones are offered by the miso broth, celery, rice, mushrooms, garlic, and parsley. The seaweed flakes are rich in extra nutrients.

2 pounds unpeeled shrimp
3¾ cups partially made miso broth (see page 150), seafood or vegetable stock (see page 151)
2 tablespoons olive oil
1 onion, chopped
2 celery stalks, chopped
2 peppers, preferably of different colors, seeded and chopped
3 garlic cloves, finely chopped
2¼ cups medium-grain rice
Two 14-ounce canned chopped plum tomatoes
1 pound chestnut mushrooms, sliced (about 5–6 cups)

2 red chiles, seeded and chopped
2 teaspoons chopped fresh thyme (or 1 teaspoon dried), plus more whole sprigs for garnishing (optional)
Handful of mixed seaweed flakes
Freshly ground sea salt and black pepper
Dash or two of no-added-sugar Worcestershire sauce
2 tablespoons chopped parsley, plus more whole leaves for garnishing

Serves 4–6

Peel the shrimp, removing the heads and tails. Drop all the trimmings into a saucepan with the miso broth (before adding the miso) or vegetable stock, and simmer gently for 20 minutes to enhance the flavor. Strain the broth (having stirred in the miso) or vegetable stock and keep hot.

Heat the oil in a large heavy-bottomed pot and sauté the onion, celery, and peppers for a few minutes until softened. Add the garlic and sauté for a minute or two more.

Stir in the rice and turn until all the grains are shiny and well coated with the oil. Pour in all the broth and add the tomatoes with their liquid, the mushrooms, and the chiles, thyme, and seaweed. Bring to a boil, stir well and season to taste with salt, pepper, and Worcestershire sauce. Cover tightly and leave to simmer very gently for 25 minutes.

Add the shrimp and parsley, cover again and simmer gently for another five minutes, or until the shrimp are nicely cooked through. Serve with more parsley leaves and more thyme sprigs if you like.

Variation: for a more elaborate garnish, keep some of the shrimp in the shell and poach them briefly in the broth until just cooked, then reserve and dot around the top of the dish when serving.

P *** E * A *****
THE MISO BROTH, CELERY, RICE, MUSHROOMS, GARLIC, AND PARSLEY PROVIDE PHYTOESTROGENS. THE SHRIMP, PEPPERS, AND TOMATOES CONTAIN ANTIOXIDANTS.

simple paella

The mussels provide EFAs and B vitamins and are rich in iron and iodine. Iodine, from natural sources, is useful at menopause as it helps to maintain the metabolism and keep the thyroid functioning at its optimum.

2 tablespoons olive oil
2 onions, chopped
2 garlic cloves, finely chopped
2 peppers, preferably of different colors, seeded and cut into thick strips
1 small head of fennel, cored and chopped, reserving any fronds for garnishing
14 ounces canned chopped plum tomatoes
Pinch of saffron strands (optional)

Freshly ground sea salt and black pepper
2 cups long-grain rice
About 3¾ cups miso broth (see page 150) or fish or seafood stock (see page 151)
Handful of mixed seaweed flakes
8 ounces peeled cooked shrimp (about 2 cups)
7 ounces canned mussels, drained
¾ cup pitted black olives
Lemon wedges, for serving

Serves 6–87

Heat the olive oil in a large deep skillet or paella pan. Sauté the onion until translucent. Add the garlic, pepper strips, and fennel, and sauté briefly until just beginning to soften.

Add the tomatoes and saffron, if using. Season to taste and bring to a boil. Add the rice, stirring in well. Pour in the broth, sprinkle in the seaweed flakes, and bring back to a boil again. Lower the heat, cover and simmer gently for about 20 minutes, until the rice is tender.

Take off the heat, mix in the shrimp, mussels, and olives, and adjust the seasoning. Add a little more broth or boiling water if necessary to moisten the paella – it should be neither sticky like a risotto nor dry like a pilaf. Cover and leave to stand for a few minutes until the seafood is thoroughly warmed through.

Serve garnished with the reserved fennel fronds, and accompanied by lemon wedges.

P *** E **** A ****

roast nut-coated cod with a lemon vinaigrette dressing

This delicious dish goes very well with Champ or Colcannon mashed potatoes (see page 113). The nuts and flaxseed oil contain Omega 3 and Omega 6 essential oils which are so good for combating premature aging.

1 tail end of cod, weighing about 1¾–2 pounds
2 tablespoons butter, plus more for greasing
Juice of 1 lemon, plus lemon slices for garnishing
Freshly ground sea salt and black pepper
Small bunch of parsley, chopped, plus more whole sprigs for garnishing
⅔ cup miso broth (see page 150) or fish stock (see page 151)

For the coating
¼ cup whole-wheat bread crumbs
2 tablespoons ground almonds
⅓ cup slivered almonds

For the lemon vinaigrette
Juice and zest of 1 lemon
2 garlic cloves, finely chopped
Small bunch of flat-leaf parsley, finely chopped, plus more whole sprigs for garnishing
⅓–½ cup olive oil
2 tablespoons flaxseed oil

Serves 4

Buy the cod with the skin left on, but get the fishmonger to scale it for you, cut it open on one side and remove the bone.

Heat the oven to 375°F and butter an ovenproof dish. Rinse the cod, including its cavity. Pat dry with paper towels. Put the fish in the prepared dish and sprinkle the lemon juice inside and outside the fish. Season lightly and sprinkle, again inside and out, with parsley. Dot the top with the butter and pour the broth around the base of the pan.

Roast for 20 minutes. Baste regularly with the liquid in the pan. After this time, mix together the coating ingredients and season well. Baste the fish and sprinkle the coating all over it. Return to the oven and cook for another 10–15 minutes, until the coating is nicely browned. Meanwhile, mix up the ingredients for the lemon vinaigrette.

Serve the fish, garnished with lemon slices and parsley sprigs, accompanied by the vinaigrette.

P ** E **** A *

pan-broiled darnes of salmon on puy lentils

This is a wonderful succulent dish, packed with phytoestrogens from the lentils as well as excellent amounts of Omega 3 fatty acids from the salmon. The seaweed flakes give extra added value with their trace mineral content. A darne is a cut piece of round fish, cut on the bone.

4 darnes (thick boneless transverse cuts) of salmon,
   each about 6–8 ounces
2 tablespoons sesame seeds, lightly toasted
Chive Butter (see page 154), for serving

For the marinade
2 tablespoons olive oil
Juice of 1 lime
2 teaspoons soy sauce
1 teaspoon mixed peppercorns
½-inch piece of fresh ginger root, very finely chopped

For the lentils
1 tablespoon olive oil
4 shallots, finely chopped
2 carrots, finely diced
⅔ cup Puy lentils
1¾ cups red wine (optional)
Large handful of mixed dried seaweed flakes
Freshly ground black pepper

Serves 4

Mix all the marinade ingredients in a large shallow dish and turn the salmon in it. Cover and leave to marinate for about an hour, turning once or twice.

Cook the lentils: heat the oil in a heavy-bottomed saucepan and sauté the shallots until translucent. Add the carrots and lentils and stir to coat well, then add the wine (if using) and seaweed. Season with pepper only. Bring to a boil, lower the heat, cover, and simmer gently for about 30–40 minutes, until all the wine is absorbed and the lentils are tender.

Towards the end of this time, lightly oil a griddle pan and preheat it. Drain the salmon pieces from the marinade and pat dry. Arrange the salmon on the hot griddle pan at an angle, cook for two minutes and flip over to cook the other side for the same time. Turn again, this time also turning the salmon through 90 degrees so that the new set of sear marks will form an attractive crosshatch (or quadrillage) on the salmon. Cook for two minutes again, then flip over again to achieve the same on the other side. During this second set of searing, check with the tip of a sharp knife to see that the salmon is cooking all the way through; if not, extend the cooking by a minute or so on each – or just the final – side.

While the fish is cooking, bring the marinade to a simmer in a small saucepan to reduce by about half.

When ready, adjust the seasoning of the lentils and spoon them onto four warmed plates. Set a piece of salmon on top of each, spoon over some of the reduced marinade, then sprinkle with the sesame seeds, and set a pat of chive butter on top of each.

P ***** E **** A **
THE LENTILS OFFER GOOD AMOUNTS OF PHYTOESTROGENS WHILE THE SALMON IS A GOOD SOURCE OF OF OMEGA 3 ESSENTIAL FATTY ACIDS.

sushi rolls

Scientists have found that seaweed is an excellent source of iodine, which keeps the thyroid gland healthy, and that seaweed can reduce cholesterol and help the more efficient metabolism of fat. Nori, sushi rice, rice vinegar, mirin (Japanese rice wine), pickled ginger, and wasabi (a type of Japanese horseradish) are sold in many healthfood stores, in some better supermarket chains, and in specialty Japanese stores. Nori is usually sold ready-toasted and perforated to make it easier to cut through after rolling. If you can't get hold of any nori, use a thick layer of lightly toasted sesame seeds as the exterior coating – the seeds will adhere to the rice. You will need a bamboo sushi mat or a double layer of waxed paper on a dish towel to roll the sushi.

7 ounces uncooked sushi rice
1 tablespoon salt
1 tablespoon mirin
3 tablespoons rice vinegar
1 tablespoon honey
2 ounces sesame seeds, very lightly toasted in a dry pan
3 sheets of toasted nori (Japanese seaweed), about 7 x 8 inches
3 tablespoons wasabi

For the fillings
About 8–10 cooked shelled tiger shrimp, butterflied open
About 4 ounces mixed fresh crab meat
About 4 ounces smoked salmon (lox), cut into strips

To serve
Dark soy sauce
Pickled ginger
More wasabi

Serves 6 (makes about 30)

Put the rice in a sieve and rinse under running cold water until the water runs clear, then drain well. Put into a large saucepan, cover with one and three-quarter cups cold water and add the salt. Cover tightly, bring to a boil and boil for one minute. Then turn the heat down and cook gently for about 15 minutes, or until all the water is absorbed and the rice is tender but still has a slight resistance to the bite. Remove from the heat and let stand, still covered, for 10 minutes.

Meanwhile, mix together the mirin, rice vinegar, and honey in a small saucepan and heat gently. Turn the rice out into a large flat plate, sprinkle over the sesame seeds and gently fold them and the dressing into the rice with a wooden spoon. Cool the rice by fanning it with a damp cloth. When the rice stops steaming, cover it with the cloth.

Place a sheet of nori, with its shiny side down and the perforations running vertically, on a sushi mat or on a double layer of waxed paper set on a clean dish towel. Spread one-third of the rice over about two-thirds of the nori, leaving a clear margin at the top, and smooth the surface.

Lay one filling in a horizontal line just off center towards the end closest to you, then smear a line of wasabi across the remaining rice just up from the filling. Pick up the mat or towel at the end closest to you, pull over the top, then push down gently with your fingers so that the end of the sushi roll tucks in and you can use the mat or towel to roll the whole thing up quite firmly, like a Swiss roll.

With a little water, dampen the bare edge of nori to help it stick. Tap the ends to neaten, leave to rest for a few minutes, then gently unroll the mat or waxed paper.

Slice the roll through the perforations or, if there aren't any, cut it into about 10 pieces. Repeat the process to make two more long rolls, each using a different filling, and cut each into pieces as before.

Serve with bowls of soy sauce and side plates with some pickled ginger and a smear of wasabi for each person.

Variations: other suggestions for fillings include strips of English cucumber, cooked spinach mixed with chopped anchovies, asparagus, avocado, salmon mousse, fresh tuna, or shiitake mushrooms lightly sautéed in olive oil.

P * E *** A **
PHYTOESTROGENS ARE AVAILABLE FROM THE RICE AND ESSENTIAL OILS FROM THE SELECTION OF FISH AND SESAME SEEDS.

broiled scallops with chile jam and crème fraîche on a potato and carrot rösti

It is worth paying that little bit extra for diver scallops, which have a much better flavor and consistency. When cooking scallops in this way, remember to take them out of the fridge some time ahead of cooking.

10–12 large fat scallops
A little olive oil, for brushing
½ cup well-chilled crème fraîche
Mixed leaves and herbs, for
   garnishing (optional)

For the chile jam
Juice and peel of 1 lime
Juice and peel of 1 small orange
6 large thin slices of fresh
   ginger root

Serves 4

1–2 hot red chiles, cut in half
   lengthwise and seeded
⅔ cup maple or date syrup

For the rösti
1 pound potatoes in their skins
1 pound carrots
Freshly ground sea salt and black
   pepper
1 tablespoon fennel seeds,
   crushed
1 tablespoon olive oil, plus more
   for greasing
2 tablespoons butter

First make the chile jam: cut the peel, ginger slices, and chile halves into thin strips. Put these in a small saucepan with the citrus juices and syrup, and stir over a low heat until simmering. Simmer for 3–4 minutes, stirring occasionally, and leave to cool. Make the rösti: cook the potatoes and carrots in boiling salted water for 10 minutes, until almost soft. Remove from the pan, and when cool enough to handle, peel away the potato skins and grate the flesh coarsely. Grate the carrots similarly. Mix these together with some seasoning and the crushed fennel seeds.

Heat the oil and butter in a large skillet until very hot. Put four oiled four-inch pastry cutters in the pan and fill these with the mixture, packing it down well. Reduce the heat and cook gently for 10 minutes.

When the undersides are nicely crisped and browned, remove each rösti from the pan by slipping a spatula under it. Carefully ease it out of the cutter mold and return it to the pan with the cooked side uppermost. Continue to cook for a further 10 minutes until the other sides are browned in the same way.

While the rösti are cooking on their second side, preheat a very hot griddle pan. Cut the scallops into two thinner discs, brush them on both sides very lightly with oil and cook them on the very hot griddle pan over a high heat for about 30–45 seconds on each side – no more as they toughen quickly! – until nicely seared and just cooked through.

Put a rösti in the center of each serving plate and spoon some crème fraîche in an uneven layer on top of each. Arrange the scallops on top of that and spoon the jam over them (you may have to warm it through again very slightly and/or let it down with a little more lime juice to get a "jammy" consistency). Serve immediately, garnished with some leaves and herbs.

P * E ** A **
SHELLFISH SUCH AS SCALLOPS ARE A GOOD SOURCE OF SELENIUM, A POWERFUL ANTIOXIDANT. PHYTOESTROGENS ARE SUPPLIED BY THE CARROTS AND POTATOES.

5

side dishes

braised fennel

This tasty, phyto-packed dish makes a good accompaniment to fish – try it with the Roast Nut-coated Cod on page 104. The phytoestrogens come from the fennel, miso broth, carrot, and garlic; the carrot provides beta-carotene.

2 large heads of fennel
Freshly ground sea salt and
  black pepper
2 tablespoons olive oil
1 small onion, sliced
1 carrot, finely diced
1–2 garlic cloves, finely chopped
Juice of ½ lemon

1¼ cups miso broth (see page 150) or vegetable stock (see page 151)
1 bouquet garni
1 tablespoon coriander seeds, crushed
Handful of mixed dried seaweed flakes
1 tablespoon butter

Serves 4

Trim the fennel, reserving any fronds. Cut the heads in half lengthwise and cut out the woody cores. Parboil the pieces of fennel for about 10 minutes in boiling salted water. Drain well and set aside.

Heat the oil in a heavy flameproof casserole or pot big enough to take the fennel in a single layer. Sauté the onion and carrot in it for a minute or two, until softened. Then add the garlic and sauté for a minute more. Stir in the lemon juice, broth, bouquet garni, coriander seeds, and seaweed and add seasoning to taste. Cover and bring slowly to a boil. Lower the heat and simmer, still covered, for about 10 minutes.

Arrange the fennel pieces, cut side down, on the bed of vegetables. Dot with the butter, cover tightly, and cook very, very gently for about 1–1½ hours, until the fennel is tender.

Remove the bouquet garni and serve garnished with the reserved fennel fronds.

Variation: you can also braise the fennel in an oven preheated to 350°F. An interesting variation on this dish is to mix the fennel with young celery hearts.

P **** E * A **

braised red cabbage with winter fruit

Red cabbage is a superb ingredient as it is valuable in the fight against cancer as well as possessing antioxidant benefits. The seaweed flakes will give you important nutrients, including iodine for a healthy thyroid. There are also plenty of different bioflavonoids in the array of fruits included here.

1 tablespoon butter
1 tablespoon olive oil
1 large onion, finely chopped
½ head of red cabbage (about 1½ pounds), shredded
5 tablespoons cider vinegar
5 tablespoons dry red wine (optional)
Large pinch of ground cinnamon
Handful of mixed seaweed flakes

1½ tablespoons honey
Juice and grated peel of 1 small orange
Juice and grated peel of 1 small lemon
1 large tart apple, diced
¾ cup seedless raisins
⅓ cup cranberries
1 teaspoon caraway seeds
Freshly ground sea salt and black pepper

Serves 4–6

Melt the butter with the oil in a large heavy-bottomed pot or casserole, add the onion, and cook gently until translucent.

Add the remaining ingredients with plenty of seasoning and mix well. Bring to a simmer, cover tightly and cook over a gentle heat for about one and a quarter hours, stirring from time to time. (You may also have to add a little more water if it shows any signs of getting too dry at any time.)

Adjust the seasoning if necessary before serving.

Variation: add some chopped boiled chestnuts to make this into a meal in itself, and to up the antioxidants (chestnuts contain vitamin E). Try the dish with the Herring with Oatmeal (see page 82), or the Roast Nut-coated Cod (see page 104).

P * E * A ****
PHYTOESTROGENS IN THE CINNAMON, CARAWAY SEEDS, AND APPLES.
THE VARIETY OF FRUITS PROVIDE BIOFLAVONOIDS, IMPORTANT ANTIOXIDANTS.

zucchini and saffron spaghetti

Just a small portion of zucchini (3½ ounces) provides you with more than a quarter of your daily needs of vitamin C. The pine nuts give you good amounts of essential oils. You have to make this dish at the very last minute to preserve its freshness and texture.

2 tablespoons butter
1 tablespoon olive oil
Pinch of saffron strands
Freshly ground sea salt and black pepper
1 pound, 5 ounces (5–6) medium to large (but not too big) young firm zucchini, unpeeled, but topped and tailed
½ cup pine nuts, lightly toasted

Serves 4

Melt the butter with the oil in a large heavy skillet over a gentle heat. Once melted, stir in the saffron and plenty of salt and pepper (enough to provide seasoning for all the zucchini once they are added). Leave over the gentlest of heats while you prepare the zucchini.

Using the shredding disc of a food processor, shred the zucchini into long spaghetti-like strands.

Turn up the heat under the skillet and, when the butter is hot, add all the zucchini strands. Working quickly, toss them with a pair of spatulas or spoons, so that all the strands are coated in the saffron butter and warmed through (you don't want them to cook all that much or they will overcook).

Serve immediately, topped with the pine nuts.

P * E ** A ***
ESSENTIAL OILS ARE PROVIDED BY THE PINE NUTS AND THE ZUCCHINI DELIVER ANTIOXIDANTS.

caponata

Caponata is the Sicilian version of ratatouille. Served cold, it makes an excellent appetizer. Nearly everything in this recipe will benefit your health. The cider vinegar and honey mix is also beneficial because it helps you absorb calcium.

2 eggplant, cut into 2-inch cubes
Sea salt and black pepper
About 3 tablespoons olive oil, plus more for greasing
1 large onion, sliced
2 large garlic cloves, finely chopped
8 ounces canned chopped plum tomatoes, liquid drained and reserved
1 bouquet garni
2 tablespoons tomato paste
1 tablespoon honey
3 tablespoons cider vinegar
2 large zucchini, cut in half lengthwise and then sliced
16 anchovies, rinsed, drained, and cut into strips
½ cup pine nuts, lightly toasted
⅓ cup salted capers, rinsed and drained
2–3 celery stalks, thinly sliced
¾ cup pitted black olives, cut into strips
About 2 tablespoons finely chopped flat-leaf parsley

Serves 4

Sprinkle the eggplant generously with salt and leave to drain in a colander for about 20 minutes. Rinse well and pat dry.

Preheat the oven to 350°F and grease a large ovenproof casserole with some of the oil.

Heat the remaining oil in a large pot and sauté the onion until translucent. Add the garlic and cook for a minute or two more. Stir in the tomatoes, bouquet garni, and tomato paste. Bring to a simmer and cook gently for about 20 minutes, until the mixture is reduced to a thick paste. Discard the bouquet garni, stir in the honey and vinegar, and simmer for a minute more.

Stir in the eggplant, zucchini, anchovies, pine nuts, capers, celery, and olives. Season to taste.

Transfer to the casserole, cover, and bake for 1½ hours, or until the vegetables are tender. Stir from time to time to prevent sticking; add some of the reserved tomato liquid if necessary. Serve warm or cool, sprinkled with finely chopped parsley.

P **** E **** A ****

colcannon

This version of the Irish classic is beautifully tasty as well as being full of goodness. If you use cabbage, you will be giving yourself extra cancer protection since the vegetable helps unwanted estrogen to be excreted in its harmless form. Using scallions as the green element gives you the other traditional mashed potato dish, champ.

2¼ pounds russet potatoes, peeled and chopped
2¼ pounds cabbage, kale, or other leafy green vegetable, shredded
1¼ cups soy milk
½ stick butter, plus more for frying
Freshly ground sea salt and black pepper

Serves 6

Cook the potatoes and greens in separate pans of boiling salted water until quite soft, about 20 minutes. Drain well.

Mash the potatoes until smooth, then beat in the greens and the milk, followed by the butter and seasoning to taste. It is traditional in Ireland not to mix in the melted butter, but to pour it into a recess made in the middle of the mixture: you then dunk forkfuls of the mash in the butter as you eat it.

Variation: you can also form the mixture into small cakes and fry these in butter until crisp and brown on both sides. For an extra phyto boost, add to the mash a spoonful or two of sesame seeds, flax seeds, or poppy seeds.

P ** E * A ****
THE SOY MILK AND POTATOES ARE THE PHYTOESTROGEN PROVIDERS IN THE DISH, AND THE GREEN VEGETABLES SUPPLY EXCELLENT LEVELS OF ANTIOXIDANTS.

brussels sprouts with peanut sauce

Brussels sprouts, like cabbage and cauliflower, belong to the cruciferous family of vegetables which helps protect against estrogen-dependent cancers of the breast and womb. This is because the indoles contained in the sprouts help to metabolize estrogen and eliminate it safely from the body.

1 pound, 2 ounces Brussels sprouts
Freshly ground sea salt
2 tablespoons soy sauce
1 recipe quantity Peanut Sauce (see page 155)
2 tablespoons olive oil
4 tablespoons pine nuts, lightly toasted

Serves 4

Cook the Brussels sprouts in boiling salted water for about five to six minutes, until just tender. Drain well.

Mix the soy sauce into the peanut sauce and set aside.

Heat the oil in a wok or large skillet, then quickly stir-fry the sprouts for two minutes. Remove from the heat and stir half the peanut sauce into the pan.

Transfer to a warmed serving dish, spoon over the remaining sauce and sprinkle with the pine nuts.

This dish makes a good accompaniment for the Tofu and Mushroom Stroganoff (see page 96), the Herby Tofu and Oat Sausages (see page 98), or the Mixed Bean and Tomato Stew (see page 95).

P * E ** A ***
BRUSSELS SPROUTS HAVE GOOD AMOUNTS OF ANTIOXIDANTS, IN THE FORM OF VITAMIN C AND BETA-CAROTENE. THE PINE NUTS ARE FULL OF EFAS.

roast root vegetables with herbs, seeds, and garlic

Serve these luxurious vegetables alongside fish for lunch and you have a banquet. Unusually, a cooked beet contains more nutrients than a raw one. These include good levels of vitamin C and potassium, which helps to control water retention.

3¼ pounds mixed root vegetables, including as many of the following as possible: potatoes, parsnips, carrots, celery root, baby turnips, beets, and shallots
1 head of garlic
⅓–½ cup olive oil
1 tablespoon honey
2 tablespoons sesame seeds
Several sprigs each of thyme and rosemary
Freshly ground sea salt and black pepper
½ cup walnut halves

Serves 4

Preheat the oven to 400°F and bring a large saucepan of salted water to a boil. Prepare the root vegetables, leaving any that are bite-sized, whole. Cut the potatoes into largish chunks and the carrots into smallish pieces (as they take longer to cook), making the rest a fairly uniform size in between. Separate the garlic into cloves, but leave them unpeeled.

Parboil all the vegetables except the garlic in the boiling water for about five minutes only. Drain well and return to the hot pan to steam dry.

In a small bowl, mix the oil with the honey, sesame seeds, herbs, and lots of seasoning. Add this to the saucepan of vegetables with the garlic and walnuts and toss to coat them all well in the mixture.

Turn the contents of the pan out into a roasting pan and roast for 45–60 minutes, shaking or stirring from time to time to help them cook uniformly, until all the vegetables are tender. (If they seem to be browning too fast before getting tender, cover them with a lid for the last part of cooking.)

P ** E * A ****
PHYTOESTROGENS SUPPLIED BY THE CARROTS, POTATOES, AND WALNUTS. THE VEGETABLES GIVE YOU PLENTY OF THE FREE RADICAL BUSTERS, ANTIOXIDANTS.

vegetable tabbouleh

My version of the classic Lebanese salad. Tabbouleh is an excellent accompaniment to broiled fish and vegetables. It also makes a fine first course (serve it with Romaine lettuce heart leaves as scoops). It is particularly good for barbecues and picnics as it keeps its taste and texture without the worry of it going soggy, as dressed leaf salads do.

1 cup bulgar wheat
1 tablespoon olive oil
1 tablespoon flaxseed oil
Juice of 3 lemons
2 garlic cloves, very finely chopped
Freshly ground sea salt and black pepper
2 large carrots
2 zucchini
Small head of broccoli
4 ounces shelled peas (about 1 cup)
Small bunch of mint, finely chopped, reserving a few whole leaves for garnishing
Large bunch of flat-leaf parsley, finely chopped reserving a few leaves for garnishing
8 ounces ripe juicy tomatoes, skinned (see page 58), stalks removed and diced
½ English cucumber, diced
1 tablespoon golden flax seeds
4–5 scallions, chopped

Serves 6–8

Put the bulgar in a large bowl and cover well with warm water. Leave for about 20 minutes to swell and soften. Drain thoroughly, squeezing to remove excess moisture, and place in a large serving bowl.

Mix the oils with the juice of two of the lemons and the garlic. Season this dressing to taste and pour it over the bulgar. Mix well and leave for about 20 minutes more.

Put a large pan of salted water on to boil. Dice the carrots,

zucchini, and broccoli to about the same size, just a little larger than the largest of the peas. Put the peas and the diced vegetables in a blanching basket and, when the water is boiling rapidly, lower into the water for one minute only. Refresh in a bowl of cold water and then drain well.

When ready to serve, mix the chopped mint and parsley into the salad, together with most of the tomatoes, the cucumber, the flax seeds, the drained blanched vegetables, and about two-thirds of the scallions. Adjust the seasoning with more salt, pepper, and lemon juice, if necessary (it should taste quite sharp).

Garnish with the remaining tomatoes and scallions and the reserved whole mint leaves and parsley leaves.

P ***** E **** A ****
PHYTO-PACKED WITH FLAX SEEDS, BULGUR WHEAT, GARLIC, CARROTS, ZUCCHINI, BROCCOLI, AND PEAS. EFAS FROM FLAXSEED OIL, ANTIOXIDANTS FROM TOMATOES.

parsley salad

It is important that you eat a variety of phytoe-strogens and that you do not come to rely on just one source, such as soy. Parsley is yet another way to feed yourself these important substances, and the dressing is also excellent for your health. This refreshingly green-tasting salad makes an ideal accompaniment to roast and broiled fish.

About 7 ounces flat-leaf parsley, leaves separated and all stalks removed

For the dressing
1 cup pitted black olives, finely chopped
1 large red onion, finely chopped
2 garlic cloves, finely chopped
About 1 tablespoon salted capers, rinsed and finely chopped

4 ripe plum tomatoes, skinned (see page 58), seeded and diced small
1 large carrot, diced small
About ½ cup extra virgin olive oil
2 tablespoons flaxseed oil
Juice and grated peel of 2 lemons
Freshly ground sea salt and black pepper

Serves 4

Mix all the ingredients for the dressing in the bottom of a glass salad bowl, with seasoning to taste.

Just before serving, throw the parsley leaves into the bowl and toss to coat them well.

Variations: serve as a first course, topped with shavings of best-quality Parmesan cheese. For a more substantial dish you could try adding anchovies, or even crumbled goat cheese.

P *** E **** A ***
PHYTOESTROGENS FROM THE PARSLEY; EFAS FROM THE FLAXSEED AND OLIVE OIL; ANTIOXIDANTS FROM THE TOMATOES AND CARROT.

caesar salad

My version of this classic is a summer salad that goes well with many robustly flavored dishes. Eggs are packed full of essential vitamins and minerals and the garlic is beneficial, both as a source of phytoestrogens and also as a booster to the immune system.

1 egg
1 large head of Romaine lettuce
Freshly ground sea salt and black pepper
4 ounces Parmesan cheese
½ cup walnut halves, lightly toasted and chopped
Garlic croutons (see page 60)

Serves 4

For the dressing
4 tablespoons olive oil
2 tablespoons flaxseed oil
2 large garlic cloves, thinly sliced
Large pinch of mustard powder
6 anchovy fillets, rinsed, drained, and finely chopped
½ teaspoon no-added-sugar Worcestershire sauce
3 tablespoons cider vinegar
Juice of 1 small lemon

The day before, put the oils for the dressing in a small bowl with the garlic slices and leave at room temperature to infuse with the garlic flavor.

Next day, when ready to serve, boil the egg for one and a half minutes only. Cool under cold running water. Shred the lettuce into a salad bowl, season well, and scoop the contents of the egg shell over the leaves.

Grate half the Parmesan. In a bowl, mix all the dressing ingredients including the garlic oil (discard the slices of garlic or use them elsewhere) and the grated Parmesan. Sprinkle the dressing over the leaves and toss well. Add in the walnuts and croutons and toss again.

Finish by shaving the remaining Parmesan into strips over the top of the salad.

P * E **** A *
GARLIC PROVIDES PHYTOESTROGENS, AND THERE IS A WONDERFUL MIX OF ESSENTIAL FATTY ACIDS FROM THE FLAXSEED OIL, ANCHOVIES, AND WALNUTS.

carrot and celery root remoulade

This refreshing and tangy salad is delicious with cold fish and seafood. It also makes a good first course for a summer's meal. Celery root, which is part of the celery family, has good amounts of potassium – an excellent mineral for helping with water retention.

1 small celery root
3–4 carrots

For the remoulade dressing
1 recipe quantity mayonnaise (see page 153)
1 tablespoon grainy mustard, or more to taste
1 tablespoon golden flax seeds
2 gherkins, very finely diced
2 tablespoons chopped herbs, including flat-leaf parsley, chives, chervil, and tarragon, plus more for garnishing
2 tablespoons capers, chopped
Freshly ground sea salt and black pepper
Dash of Tabasco
Juice of 1–2 lemons, according to taste

Serves 6–8

Bring a large pan of salted water to a boil. Grate the vegetables into long strands and put these into the boiling water. Boil for two minutes only, then drain and plunge immediately into a bowl of cold water to stop the cooking process. Drain thoroughly and pat dry using a clean cloth or paper towels.

While the vegetables are cooking and draining, make the remoulade dressing by mixing all the ingredients together and seasoning with salt, pepper, Tabasco, and lemon juice.

In a large bowl, toss the vegetables in the dressing, adjusting the seasoning if necessary, and sprinkle with herbs to serve.

P ** E ** A **
THE CARROTS CONTAIN THE ANTIOXIDANT BETA-CAROTENE, AND ALONG WITH THE FLAX SEEDS BRING PHYTOESTROGENS. THE LATTER ALSO BRINGS EFAS.

fattoush

Fattoush is a wonderful Syrian bread salad. Not only do the flax seeds (and their oil) contain phytoe-strogens – as do the parsley, garlic, and soy yogurt – but also essential fatty acids. These essential oils help keep your hormones in balance and your skin and hair soft. Both the peppers and tomatoes are rich in antioxidants and so help disarm free radicals.

2 large flat pita breads
Juice of 2–3 large lemons
1 large red onion, finely chopped
6 large ripe vine-ripened tomatoes, chopped
1 English cucumber, diced
2 small peppers, preferably of different colors, seeded and finely diced
1 garlic clove, finely chopped
1/3–1/2 cup olive oil
2 tablespoons flaxseed oil
About 6 tablespoons finely chopped flat-leaf parsley
About 2 tablespoons finely chopped cilantro leaves
About 2 tablespoons finely chopped mint leaves
1 tablespoon golden flax seeds
Freshly ground sea salt and black pepper
Pomegranate seeds, for garnishing (optional)
Soy yogurt, for serving (optional)

Serves 4

Open out the pita breads and toast them lightly on both sides, then break them up into bite-sized pieces.

Just before you want to serve the salad, put all the ingredients, including the pita, in a large glass salad bowl and toss well. Season to taste and add more lemon juice if necessary.

Serve immediately, garnished with pomegranate seeds if you choose and with soy yogurt on the side.

P **** E *** A ***
PHYTOESTROGENS FROM THE FLAX SEEDS, PARSLEY, GARLIC, AND SOY YOGURT. EFAS FROM FLAX SEEDS AND THEIR OIL; ANTIOXIDANTS FROM PEPPERS AND TOMATOES.

austrian bean salad with tofu dressing

The delicious tofu dressing and unusual marriage of apples and gherkins with the beans makes for an extremely tasty and pretty dish. The various beans give you plenty of fiber as well as phytoestrogens. The dressing is made with beneficial linseed oil as well as olive oil, which is good for a healthy heart.

6 ounces canned or cooked red kidney beans
6 ounces canned or cooked flageolet beans
6 ounces canned or cooked borlotti or cannellini beans
4 ounces cooked waxy potatoes, diced
2 sharp firm eating apples, cored and diced
3 ounces sweet gherkins, finely diced
1 tablespoon dill or fennel fronds, chopped, plus more for garnishing

For the tofu dressing
9 ounces tofu
3 tablespoons cider vinegar
2 tablespoons olive oil
1 tablespoon flaxseed oil
1 teaspoon English mustard
1 tablespoon honey
Freshly ground sea salt and black pepper

Serves 4–6

Make the tofu dressing by blending all the ingredients in a food processor until smooth and seasoning to taste. If you are cooking the beans yourself, see the advice on cooking beans in the Shopping and Cooking Tips (page 40).

Put all the other ingredients in a large, preferably glass, salad bowl and pour over the dressing. Make sure you dress the drained beans while they are still warm so that the dressing really soaks in. Toss lightly to mix so that all the ingredients are lightly coated in the dressing but are still identifiable.

Serve garnished with more dill or fennel leaves.

P ***** E *** A *
THE SELECTION OF BEANS, PLUS THE APPLES AND POTATOES, OFFER PLENTY OF PHYTOESTROGENS. EFAS COME FROM THE FLAXSEED OIL AND OLIVE OIL.

cinnamon rice with nuts and raisins

This is a lovely way to serve rice and a simple version of jeweled rice. For added benefits you can buy organic brown basmati rice. Rice is a source of phytoestrogens, as is the cinnamon. The almonds will provide you with some essential oils.

1¼ cups basmati rice
Freshly ground sea salt
3-inch piece of cinnamon stick
2–3 bay leaves
2 ounces seedless raisins (about ⅓ cup)
2 tablespoons slivered almonds, lightly toasted

Serves 6–8

Rinse the rice thoroughly in a sieve and, if you have time, soak in plenty of fresh cold water for about 30 minutes.

Bring one and three-quarter cups of water to the boil in a large pot. Add salt to taste, the cinnamon stick, and the bay leaves. Bring back to a boil and add the drained rice. Stir well, reduce the heat to the barest simmer, cover tightly, and cook for 10 minutes.

Take off the heat and leave without touching the lid for another 10 minutes.

After 10 minutes, remove the cinnamon and bay leaves. Mix in the raisins and nuts, and fluff up with a fork.

P ** E ** A *
PHYTOESTROGENS ARE PRESENT IN THE RICE AND THE CINNAMON. EFAS ARE SUPPLIED BY THE ALMONDS.

6

desserts

minted fruit salad

This salad also makes a perfect first course on a warm summer's day. Obviously, the mix of fruit used in the salad can be adjusted according to season. This particular combination of pretty berries and firm-fleshed fruit gives the dish excellent anti-aging and anti-cancer benefits. The addition of mint lends it a fresh, leafy tang.

Juice of 1 lemon
5 tablespoons honey
2 tablespoons fresh mint leaves, finely chopped, plus more whole leaves for decorating
2 oranges
8 ounces seedless black grapes (about 1⅓ cups)
2 ripe pears
2 ripe firm-fleshed apples
2 bananas
1 small ripe melon
8 ounces mixed berry fruit in season, such as strawberries, raspberries, blueberries
Soy yogurt or cream, for serving

Serves 6–8

Mix the lemon juice, honey, and chopped mint in the bottom of a large bowl. As you prepare the fruit, stir it into this mixture, trying to add any juices to the bowl. Peel the oranges and then cut down into each segment to release the flesh from its envelope of skin; cut the grapes in half, if large; cut in half and core the unpeeled pears and apples and then cut into bite-sized chunks; peel and slice the bananas; cut in half and seed the melon and scoop out the flesh using a melon baller or sharp-edged teaspoon. Chill for at least an hour.

Just before serving, mix in the berry fruit and decorate with sprigs of mint. Serve with soy yogurt or cream.

Variation: to boost the phytoestrogen content, you could sprinkle a couple of tablespoons of flax seeds into the salad with the berry fruit, or add some freshly squeezed juice from a lump of ginger root (chop finely and squeeze in a piece of cheesecloth or in a garlic press.)

P **** E **** A *****
THE SOY YOGURT GIVES PHYTOESTROGENS, ADDED TO BY LINSEEDS, IF SPRINKLED IN. FLAX SEEDS CONTAIN BOTH OMEGA 3 AND OMEGA 6 EFAS.

fruit kabobs

The soy yogurt supplies phytoestrogens and the almonds are full of essential oils. The fruit offers a variety of powerful antioxidants which combat free radicals and prevent premature aging.

2 pounds assorted firm fruit such as apples, pears, plums, grapes, cherries, persimmon, figs, peaches, nectarines, strawberries, apricot, mango, papaya
Juice of 1–2 lemons
1/3 cup slivered almonds, plus more for garnishing

Yogurt, preferably soy yogurt, for serving

For the ginger and cinnamon butter
2-inch piece of ginger root
½ stick unsalted butter, softened
2 tablespoons maple syrup
1 teaspoon ground cinnamon

Serves 4

Soak eight small wooden skewers in water, so they won't burn during cooking. Preheat a hot broiler or light a barbecue.

As appropriate, core, seed, and pit the fruit, leaving smaller fruit whole and cutting the larger fruit into large bite-sized chunks. Leave edible skins on as they will help hold the cooking fruit together. As you work, sprinkle the cut fruit with lemon juice to prevent discoloration. Arrange the prepared fruit attractively on the skewers.

Make the ginger cinnamon butter: squeeze the juice from the ginger (use a garlic press or piece of cheesecloth) into a small bowl, add the remaining ingredients, and mash together.

Using a pastry brush, coat the fruit on the skewers liberally with the butter, and sprinkle with the almonds. Grill or barbecue the kabobs for about one and a half to two minutes on each side, basting them fairly constantly with more of the ginger cinnamon butter or the pan juices.

Serve immediately, sprinkled with any remaining butter or pan juices and almonds, accompanied by yogurt.

P *** E * A ****
PHYTOESTROGENS ARE PROVIDED BY THE SOY YOGURT AND ANTIOXIDANTS ARE PRESENT IN THE FRUIT. ALMONDS ARE A GOOD SOURCE OF ESSENTIAL OILS.

stuffed pears in red wine

Pears have such a delicate flavor; their marriage with red wine here delivers high amounts of antioxidants – so good for preventing premature aging – and the soy yogurt provides phytoestrogens.

2 tablespoons golden raisins
1 tablespoon cider vinegar
1 lemon
4 large firm pears
1¼ cups red wine

3 tablespoons honey
1 cinnamon stick
1 level tablespoon black peppercorns
Soy yogurt, for serving

Serves 4

At least two hours before you intend to cook the pears, put the golden raisins in a small bowl and pour over the vinegar and the juice of half the lemon. Toss to mix well.

Peel the pears and halve them carefully lengthwise, leaving the stalks attached to one half. Scoop out the cores.

Pour the red wine into a saucepan just big enough to hold the pear halves snugly. Heat gently and stir in the honey, cinnamon, peppercorns, and three tablespoons of the remaining lemon juice. When the honey has dissolved, put the pears in the liquid and spoon some over their tops. Cover and poach at the gentlest possible simmer for 15–20 minutes, turning the pears from time to time and spooning liquid over them, until the pears are translucent and tender but still quite firm.

Remove the pears to a serving dish and strain the liquid. When the pears are cool enough to handle, stuff the cavities of four of the pear halves with a mounded spoonful of the macerated sultanas. Reassemble with the other matching pear half and wrap tightly in waxed paper. Put the pear packages and liquid to chill in the fridge for at least two to three hours.

To serve, unwrap the packages and spoon over some of the reserved poaching liquid. Serve with some yogurt flavored with a couple of spoonfuls of the poaching liquid.

P *** E * A ***
THE SOY YOGURT IS A GOOD SOURCE OF PHYTOESTROGENS AND THE PEARS AND RED WINE SUPPLY ANTIOXIDANTS.

mixed berry fool

Mixed berries contain proanthocyanidins, which are excellent antioxidants. They are useful in preventing osteoporosis since they stop the destruction of collagen and strengthen the collagen matrix. With their powerful antioxidant properties, they also play a major part in the prevention of heart disease and strokes.

1 pound mixed berries of the season
8 ounces soft tofu, chilled
Dash of vanilla extract
Maple syrup to taste
A little soy milk, chilled

Serves 4

Reserving a few of each type of berry for decoration, put all the ingredients except the soy milk in a blender or food processor. Process well until smooth.

If too thick, let down with a little soy milk if necessary to give a good consistency (it should be like cream that has been whipped to soft peaks.)

Spoon into clear glasses and decorate with the reserved berries. Chill briefly before serving.

Variation: if you have the time, puree half the berries on their own with some maple syrup to taste and build up layers of fool and puree in the glasses for a really attractive effect.

P **** E * A *****
PLENTY OF PHYTOESTROGENS FROM THE TOFU AND SOY MILK, AND THE MIXED BERRIES PROVIDE ANTIOXIDANTS.

summer pudding with elderflower yogurt

The elderflower tea is an anti-inflammatory for the joints, the soy yogurt contains plant hormones, and the berries are an excellent store of antioxidants.

6–8 thick slices of day-old whole-wheat bread
1¾ pounds mixed fruits, mostly raspberries and red currants and some of the following: strawberries, blueberries, seedless cherries, blackberries, or loganberries

4–5 tablespoons runny honey

For the elderflower yogurt
1 sachet (1 heaped tablespoon) of elderflower tea
1 cup soy yogurt
2 tablespoons runny honey

Serves 6–8

Remove the crusts from the bread and use most of the slices to line the bottom and sides of a one-and-a half pint dessert dish, cutting the bread to get a good fit if necessary.

Put all the fruit in a large heavy-bottomed saucepan and drizzle over the honey. Put over a very low heat. Cook for 3–4 minutes only, stirring carefully from time to time until the juices just begin to run but the fruit is not losing any of its shape.

Remove the pan from the heat and spoon the fruit and juices into the lined dish, reserving 2–3 tablespoons of the juices. Cover the pudding with more pieces of bread cut to fit and place a small plate with a diameter just less than that of the rim of the dish on top of the pudding. Weigh this down with a couple of cans. Chill for 3–4 hours, or preferably overnight.

Make the elderflower yogurt: put the elderflower tea in a heatproof bowl and pour two tablespoons of boiling water over it. Leave to steep for about 15 minutes. Put the yogurt in another bowl, strain in the elderflower infusion and stir in the honey, and chill. When ready to serve, remove the weights and plate and turn the pudding out on a serving plate. Trickle over the reserved juices, taking care to cover any patches of the bread crust which are still pale. Serve cut in wedges, with some of the elderflower yogurt.

P *** E * A ****
THE SOY YOGURT CONTAINS PLENTY OF PHYTOESTROGENS AND ALL THE BERRIES ARE AN EXCELLENT SOURCE OF ANTIOXIDANTS.

mixed berry soufflé omelet

Eggs are full of nutrients and, even though they are high in cholesterol, studies have shown that they do not increase cholesterol levels in the body. The tofu cream in this omelet gives excellent phytoestrogen levels and the berries are a great source of anti-aging and anti-cancer antioxidants.

3 tablespoons honey
Pinch of ground cinnamon
5 tablespoons crème fraîche or Tofu Cream (see page 155)
6 large eggs
1 tablespoon lemon juice
Freshly ground black pepper
8 ounces mixed berry fruit such as raspberries, blueberries, and strawberries
2 tablespoons butter

Serves 4–6

In a large bowl, mix half the honey and the cinnamon into the crème fraîche or tofu cream. Separate the eggs, beat the yolks lightly and mix into the cream mixture.

In a small bowl, mix the remaining honey and the lemon juice with a grinding of black pepper. When they are well mixed, add the berries, and toss to coat them well.

In another (very clean and dry) large bowl, beat the egg whites until standing in stiff peaks. Take two or three large spoonfuls of this and add to the cream mixture. Mix well to loosen the mixture. Then add the remaining egg whites and fold in lightly but thoroughly, using the side of a large metal spoon.

Put a flameproof serving dish in to warm (but don't let it get too hot) and heat a fairly hot broiler. Melt the butter in a large heavy skillet over medium heat.

When the butter is just on the point of turning color, add the cream mixture and cook over a low to medium heat until the edges start to puff. Shake the pan from time to time. When the omelet starts to move freely around in the pan, spoon the berries over one half of the omelet, making sure they go right out to the edge so they can be glimpsed when the omelet is folded. Fold the other side of the omelet over the fruit and slide it out onto the warmed serving dish.

Place under the broiler and cook until well risen, then serve at once, cutting into wedges at the table.

P *** E ** A ****

banana cream pie

This seems a wicked pie but actually does not have the usual fat-laden cream and eggs, proving that you can have your pie and eat it. The filling is set with agar, a seaweed which comes in white flakes and contains a number of excellent nutrients including iodine. Iodine is necessary for healthy thyroid function and has anti-cancer benefits.

For the crust
3 tablespoons corn oil
4 tablespoons maple syrup
1½ cups whole-wheat flour

Serves 4–6

For the filling
1 tablespoon arrowroot
2½ cups soy milk
3 tablespoons agar seaweed
3 tablespoons maple syrup
Grated peel of 1 orange
½ teaspoon vanilla extract
2 ripe bananas, very thinly sliced

Preheat the oven to 350°F.

First make the crust: mix the oil and syrup in a blender or food processor and pour into a mixing bowl. Mix in the flour and rub in with the fingertips until fully mixed and a crumbly consistency. Compact the mixture into the base and up the sides of a 9-inch pie dish. Allow to cool.

Make the filling: in a small bowl, mix the arrowroot with two tablespoons of the soy milk and set aside. Put the remaining soy milk, agar, maple syrup and orange peel in a saucepan, bring to a simmer, and cook gently for three minutes. Add the arrowroot solution and continue to cook, stirring constantly, until thick. Remove from the heat.

Stir in the vanilla, followed by the banana slices. Pour the mixture into the cooled crust and then chill for one hour, or until set.

P **** E * A *
PHYTOESTROGENS ARE SUPPLIED BY THE SOY MILK, WHOLE-WHEAT FLOUR, AND ORANGE ZEST.

clafoutis

A French dish, clafoutis is traditionaly made with cherries but you could use any seasonal fruit including pears, apples, and apricots. This version is marvelously simple to make, and quite delicious as well as healthy. The soy milk gives a good supply of plant hormones and the cherries contain useful antioxidants.

2 tablespoons butter
1 cup all-purpose flour
2 teaspoon freshly ground sea salt
1¼ cups soy milk
4 eggs
3 tablespoons honey
⅓–½ cup kirsch
1 pound ripe tart black cherries

Serves 6

Preheat the oven to 350°F and put a shallow baking dish containing the butter in the oven.

In a large bowl, mix the flour, salt, milk, eggs, honey, and kirsch to a smooth batter.

When the oven is at the right temperature, take out the hot dish and tilt it at all angles to coat it well with the melted butter. Pour in the batter, then sprinkle the cherries into the batter and return to the oven for about 35–40 minutes, until well puffed-up and colored.

Serve warm, and don't worry that it sinks as it cools – this is normal.

Variation: you can also make this dessert using seedless black cherries from a can – make sure you drain them first.

P *** E * A ***
GOOD AMOUNTS OF PLANT HORMONES FROM THE SOY MILK, AND THE CHERRIES PROVIDE ANTIOXIDANTS.

fruit tart

If you are short of time you can buy ready-made whole-wheat pastry crusts in healthfood stores. Of course, they are never as good as the homemade variety but the ingredients are healthy. However, bought pastry does not contain soy flour, which this recipe does. Essential oils are present in the nuts and sesame seeds and good levels of antioxidants in the fruit.

8 ounces plums, cut in half and pitted
3–4 firm dessert apples, cut in half, cored, and sliced
2–3 large ripe bananas, peeled and sliced

For the pastry dough
1 cup all-purpose, preferably whole-wheat flour
¼ cup soy flour
Large pinch of freshly ground salt

Serves 6–8

1½ sticks soft unsalted butter, diced small
2 egg yolks
2 tablespoons honey
Peel of 1 small orange, grated

For the glaze
4 tablespoons maple syrup
½ stick butter
1 cup cashew nuts or macadamia nuts, lightly toasted and coarsely chopped
2 tablespoons sesame seeds, lightly toasted

Make the pastry dough: sift the flours and salt into a large bowl, make a well in the center and add the diced butter. Mix in lightly. In a small bowl, beat the egg yolks lightly with the honey and three tablespoons of water. Add this to the flour mixture with the orange peel. Work the ingredients together with the fingertips until it coheres (you may need a very little more water). Roll into a ball and knead briefly and lightly.

Roll out on a lightly floured surface and use to line a 10-inch shallow tart pan. Leave to rest in the refrigerator for a short while. Preheat the oven to 375°F.

Arrange the fruit decoratively on the tart bottom: concentric circles with the plum halves, cut side down, in the center, the apple around them and the bananas around the outside look

good. Bake for 25–30 minutes until the crust is a deep color and the fruit is tender when pierced.

Meanwhile make the glaze by mixing the maple syrup and butter in a heavy-based saucepan. As soon as it comes to a boil, stop stirring, and allow it to simmer until it starts to thicken. Remove from the heat and dip the base of the pan in cold water to stop the cooking process. Keep warm.

When the tart comes out of the oven, pour the glaze uniformly over the top, and sprinkle with the nuts and seeds. Serve warm.

P** E*** A***
PHYTOESTROGENS FROM THE SOY FLOUR, PLUMS, AND APPLES; EFAS FROM THE NUTS AND SESAME SEEDS; ANTIOXIDANTS PRESENT IN THE FRUIT.

apricot tofu ice cream

Apricots are an excellent source of beta-carotene, one of the most important antioxidants. They also contain potassium, which helps reduce high blood pressure and water retention. Make sure the dried apricots are free from sulphur dioxide – they will look brown but still taste great. The tofu supplies a high degree of plant hormones.

1¾ cups apple juice
2 tablespoons agar agar seaweed
1 cup dried apricots, stewed, drained, and cooled
1 pound soft tofu

Serves 6

Pour the apple juice into a saucepan and sprinkle over the agar agar. Bring to a simmer and cook gently until the agar agar is dissolved, a few minutes.

Pour into a blender or food processor and add the apricots and tofu. Blend until smooth.

Freeze until firm but not solid, about one hour. Leave to soften in the fridge for 15 minutes before serving.

P **** E * A ****
PLENTY OF PHYTOESTROGENS IN THE TOFU, AND THE APRICOTS PROVIDE GOOD AMOUNTS OF ANTIOXIDANTS.

tofu cheesecake

Not strictly speaking a cheesecake, this dish uses tofu instead of dairy and, of course, delivers the health benefits of the phytoestrogens in the tofu. Use soft silken tofu for this recipe as it is easier to mix with other ingredients. The sesame seed paste (tahini) gives an excellent amount of calcium.

1 pie crust (see Banana Cream Pie, page 128)

For the filling
Four 8-ounce packs of soft tofu
4–8 tablespoons maple syrup, to taste
6 tablespoons tahini
1 teaspoon vanilla extract
2 teaspoons lemon juice
Pinch of freshly ground sea salt

Serves 4–6

Preheat the oven to 350°F.

Make the filling: crumble the tofu into a blender or food processor. Add the remaining ingredients and blend until smooth.

Pour into the pie crust and bake for 35–40 minutes, until the pastry is a light golden brown. Allow to cool before serving.

P **** E * A *
THE TOFU PROVIDES THE PHYTOESTROGENS IN THIS DISH, AND THE TAHINI DELIVERS THE ESSENTIAL FATTY ACIDS.

atholl brose

This aristocratic dessert is said to have been invented by and named after a Duke of Atholl. Oats are excellent for the heart because they naturally contain oat bran and are also a source of phytoestrogens. This dish is a perfect vehicle for using them in something other than a breakfast cereal. Use the whisky for very special occasions only.

⅔ cup fine oatmeal, toasted
4 tablespoons good honey, preferably
   heather honey, plus more for serving
1¼ cup soy cream
6 tablespoons Scotch whisky (optional)

Serves 4

Mix the oatmeal and honey into the soy cream and chill well. Stir in the whisky (if using) just before serving, topped with another spoonful of the honey.

P **** E * A *
PHYTOESTROGENS IN GOOD SUPPLY FROM THE OATS, AND INCREASED BY THE SOY CREAM.

baked figs

Figs contain pectin, a soluble fiber, which is good for the bowels and also helps to lower cholesterol levels. They also contain an enzyme called ficin, which aids digestion, and are a good source of calcium. The soy yogurt provides the phytoestrogens in this dessert and the pistachio nuts bring essential oils.

18 ripe figs
⅔ cup pistachio nuts, coarsely chopped,
   reserving a few for decoration
4 tablespoons honey
Peel of 1 large orange, grated
¾ cup soy yogurt

Serves 6

Preheat the oven to 400°F.

Shave off a thin sliver from the fat end of each fig so they will sit upright without falling over. Cut a cross in the top end of each fig, to about halfway down. Ease the figs open, squeezing the bottom halves if necessary.

Mix together the chopped pistachios and honey. Spoon this mixture into the figs and bake for about 15 minutes. Allow to cool slightly.

In a small bowl, mix the orange peel into the yogurt. Spoon this into the figs and decorate with the reserved pistachios before serving warm.

P *** E ** A *
THE SOY YOGURT IS AN EXCELLENT SOURCE OF PHYTOESTROGENS AND EFAS ARE PRESENT IN THE PISTACHIO NUTS.

strawberry shortcake

The queen of the summer fruits, the strawberry is also an excellent source of antioxidants. It contains more vitamin C than any other berry so it is very good for the immune system and also helps to produce collagen for skin and bone health. The shortcake's phytoestrogen content is also very high.

½ cup strawberries, cut in half or thickly sliced (depending on size)
3 tablespoons maple syrup
Squeeze of lemon juice

For the shortcake dough
1 cup whole-wheat flour
2 cups all-purpose flour, plus more for dusting
2 heaped tablespoons soy flour
1 tablespoon baking powder
Pinch of freshly ground salt
6 tablespoons cold unsalted butter, diced, plus more for glazing
3 tablespoons honey, plus more for glazing
⅔ cup soy milk

For the filling
10 ounces silken tofu
2 tablespoons honey
1 unwaxed orange, finely grated
2 tablespoons brandy
2 tablespoons vanilla extract

Serves 8

In a bowl, gently toss the strawberry slices in the maple syrup and lemon juice. Set aside to macerate for at least two hours, tossing from time to time.

Towards the end of this time, make the shortcakes: preheat the oven to 450°F. Sift the flours, baking powder, and salt into a large bowl. Add the butter and, using your fingers, rub into the flour until the mixture resembles coarse crumbs. Add the honey and all but a spoonful or two of the soy milk. Stir gently until a dough forms; if it is too thick (it should be soft but not too sloppy), add the remaining milk.

With floured hands and on a floured surface, roll it into a ball and knead for about 30 seconds. Then pat out to a round about three-quarters of an inch thick. Using a 2¾-inch pastry cutter, cut out rounds, re-rolling as necessary to get eight rounds. Arrange on a baking sheet, spaced well apart.

In a pan melt a little butter, then mix in some honey and brush the tops of the rounds as a glaze. Bake for about 10–12 minutes until well risen and golden. Transfer to a wire rack to cool until they are no longer hot, but warm.

Make the filling: in a blender or food processor, blend together all the ingredients until smooth and slightly aerated.

Split each of the warm shortcakes across into two halves and spread the bottom halves with a little of the filling. Arrange a thick layer of strawberry slices on top of each and then cover generously with filling. Put the shortcake top halves in place on top, cover with another thick layer of filling, strawberry slices, and more filling if there is any left. Arrange any remaining strawberry slices decoratively around the shortcakes, pour the strawberry juices around the plates and serve immediately.

P **** E ** A ***
THE WHOLE-WHEAT FLOUR, SOY FLOUR, SOY MILK, AND TOFU CREAM BRING PHYTOESTROGENS. ANTIOXIDANTS IN THE STRAWBERRIES.

breads, cakes, and cookies

four-seed loaf

This loaf contains lots of beneficial seeds such as sesame seeds, flax seeds, and poppy seeds. The small quantity of honey will give the bread a slightly sweet taste and the seeds will provide lovely texture. Allow about 30 minutes preparation time, plus 2½ hours' rising. This is delicious warmed up for breakfast.

1 ounce sesame seeds
1 ounce flax seeds
1 ounce poppy seeds
1 ounce sunflower seeds
½ ounce fresh yeast
1 tablespoon honey
1¾ cups lukewarm water
3 cups unbleached white bread flour, plus more
    for sprinkling and dusting
2¾ cups whole-wheat bread flour
½ tablespoon sea salt
1 tablespoon olive oil, plus more for greasing

Makes 1 large loaf

Mix the seeds together in a bowl and set aside. Crumble the yeast into another small bowl and mix with the honey and four tablespoons of the lukewarm water until smooth.

Mix the flours and three-quarters of the mixed seeds together with the salt in a large mixing bowl. Make a well in the center and tip in the yeast mixture, followed by the rest of the lukewarm water and the olive oil. Draw a little flour in from the edge until you have a smooth thick batter in the well. Sprinkle the surface of the batter with a little flour and leave for about 20 minutes, until the batter is spongy.

Gradually mix the remaining flour from the outside edges into the batter and work until it gathers into a ball, leaving the sides of the bowl clean. Turn out on to a lightly floured surface and knead for about 10 minutes, turning it as you do so, so it is stretched in different directions. Shape again into a smooth ball, put in an oiled bowl and turn to coat it with the oil. Cover with a damp dish towel and leave to rise in a draft-free place for about one to one and a half hours, or until doubled in size (it is perfectly risen when it doesn't spring back when pressed).

Using the knuckles, knock the dough back in the bowl, then turn out on the floured surface and shape it into a round or oval as you wish. Sprinkle the remaining seeds over the surface and roll the loaf in them to coat it, pressing the seeds in with your hands if necessary. Place on a baking sheet, cover with a damp dish towel and leave to rise again for about one hour, until doubled in size.

Preheat the oven to 425°F.

Uncover the loaf and cut a deep cross in the center if round or diagonal slashes across the top if oval. Bake the loaf for 15 minutes, until lightly browned, then reduce the oven setting to 375°F and bake for 20–25 minutes more, until the loaf sounds hollow when the base is tapped.

Let cool on a wire rack.

P **** E **** A *
SEEDS PROVIDE BOTH PHYTOESTROGENS AND ESSENTIAL OILS; FLAX SEEDS CONTAIN BOTH OMEGA 3 AND OMEGA 6 OILS.

corn bread

This traditional bread from the South works well in both a sweet and savory context. It is good spread with no-added-sugar jelly or as an accompaniment to dishes such as Hoppin' John (see page 96). Corn is a source of potassium and the soy milk and caraway seeds provide phytoestrogens.

Olive oil or butter for greasing
⅔ cup whole-wheat flour
1 cup fine yellow cornmeal
2½ teaspoons double-acting baking powder
¾ teaspoon salt
2 eggs
1–2 tablespoons honey
3 tablespoons butter, melted
1 cup soy milk
2 teaspoons caraway seeds

Makes a 9-in square loaf

Preheat the oven to 425°F and grease a nine-inch square cake pan. Put it in the oven to heat.

Sift the flour, cornmeal, baking powder, and salt into a large bowl and make a well in the center. In another small bowl, beat the eggs, then beat into them the honey and melted butter, followed by the milk. Pour this into the well in the flours and combine quickly with a few stirs until a smooth batter. Stir in the caraway seeds.

Pour into the hot pan, smooth the top and return to the oven. Bake for 20–25 minutes, until golden and firm to the touch. Serve, cut into squares.

P *** E ** A *
THE SOY MILK AND CARAWAY SEEDS ARE A GOOD SOURCE OF PHYTOE-STROGENS; THE SEEDS ALSO PROVIDE ESSENTIAL OILS.

seed rolls

There are lots of plant estrogens in these rolls, particularly from the flax seeds but also from the other seeds and soy milk. Essential oils are supplied by the seeds.

½ ounce flax seeds
½ ounce sesame seeds
½ ounce poppy seeds
About 2 cups unbleached all-purpose white bread flour, plus more for sprinkling and dusting
1½ cups whole-wheat flour
1 heaped teaspoon ground sea salt
1 heaped teaspoon butter, diced, plus more for greasing
1 tablespoon honey
About 1¼ cups warm soy milk
½ ounce fresh yeast

Makes about 8

Mix all the flax seeds with three-quarters of the sesame and poppy seeds. Set aside. Sift the flours and salt into a large mixing bowl. Rub the butter into the flour with the fingertips. Blend in the reserved seed mix and make a well in the center. In another bowl, mix the honey into the milk and crumble the yeast into it. Mix well until dissolved. Pour the yeast mixture into the well in the flours and mix to a soft batter, beating until it leaves the sides of the bowl clean (you may have to add a little more white flour).

Shape into a round, put in a buttered bowl and turn to coat it in the butter. Cover with a dish towel and leave to rise until doubled in size, about an hour.

Knead into a long cylinder and cut this into about eight pieces. Roll each into a sphere. Sprinkle the surface with the remaining poppy and sesame seeds and roll each sphere over them to cover the sides and top. Set well apart on a baking sheet and leave again to rise until doubled in size, about 30 minutes.

Preheat the oven to 450°F. Bake the rolls for about 40 minutes, until golden and sounding hollow when tapped on their bases. Allow to cool on wire racks.

P **** E *** A *

phyto bars

These make good energy-giving snacks at any time of day, as well as delivering good quantities of phytoestrogens. They are perfect for carrying with you for whenever your blood sugar begins to drop. This recipe has a good level of plant hormones from all the seeds (the linseeds in particular) and, of course, essential fatty acids.

Olive oil and butter for greasing
1 pound honey
1 tablespoon lemon juice
3 ounces sesame seeds, lightly toasted
3 ounces sunflower seeds, lightly toasted
3 ounces poppy seeds
3 ounces flax seeds

Makes about 12

Lightly grease the insides of a large heavy-bottomed saucepan and butter a Swiss roll pan.

Put the honey and lemon juice in the saucepan, mix well and bring to a boil (without any further stirring) over medium heat. Then, stirring constantly, boil to a temperature of 280°F to "soft crack stage" (a little of the syrup dropped into ice water stretches into hard but elastic strands). Immediately take off the heat and stir in all the seeds, combining well, then quickly pour into the prepared Swiss roll pan and set aside.

After it has cooled for about 10 minutes, use a wetted knife to mark it into about 12 bars. When completely cool, cut or break the bars apart. Store in an airtight container, interleaved with waxed paper to prevent sticking.

P **** E **** A *
PLENTY OF PHYTOESTROGENS AND ESSENTIAL FATTY ACIDS FROM ALL THE SEEDS, ESPECIALLY THE FLAX SEEDS.

deluxe pancakes

Blissfully quick to make, pancakes make a perfect coffee-time or mid-morning treat and are full of nutritious ingredients such as flax seeds and almonds. Choose dried apricots without sulphur dioxide, which is a preservative that occurs naturally, but is produced chemically for commercial use.

1 stick butter, plus more for greasing
6 tablespoons apple concentrate
1 tablespoon flax seeds
1 tablespoon sunflower seeds
1 tablespoon sesame seeds
½ teaspoon ground cinnamon
½ teaspoon ground ginger
2½ cups rolled oats
1 tablespoon slivered almonds
½ cup seedless raisins, chopped
⅓ cup no-need-to-soak dried apricots, chopped

Makes about 20

Preheat the oven to 350°F and butter a Swiss roll pan.

In a small saucepan over low heat, melt the butter with the apple concentrate, seeds, and spices. Stir in the oats, nuts, and fruit, and mix well.

Spread the mixture about ¼–½ inches thick in the prepared pan and bake for about 15–20 minutes, until golden.

Allow to cool slightly and then mark into rectangles with a knife and break into pieces. Allow to cool completely.

P **** E **** A *
PHYTOESTROGENS PROVIDED BY THE SEEDS AND OATS; EFAS FROM THE SEEDS AND ALMONDS. THE APRICOTS CONTAIN THE ANTIOXIDANT BETA-CAROTENE.

banana bread

Banana bread has no need for added sugar as it is naturally sweet. The addition of apricots and nuts makes this recipe especially delicious. Bananas are an excellent fruit as they are high in both potassium (useful with water retention) and pectin, which is a soluble fiber that can help lower cholesterol.

Butter or olive oil for greasing
½ stick slightly salted butter
½ cup date syrup
Peel of 1 lemon, finely grated
2 eggs, lightly beaten
3 large ripe (or overripe) bananas, mashed
1½ cups whole-wheat self-rising flour
2 tablespoons soy flour
½ cup pecan nuts or walnuts, chopped
½ cup dried apricots, chopped

Makes 1 medium loaf

Preheat the oven to 375°F and grease a large loaf pan.

In a large mixing bowl, cream the butter with the syrup and lemon peel, then beat in the eggs followed by the banana puree. Sift in one-third of the mixed flours and beat until smooth, then add the rest of the flours in the same way. Fold in the nuts and fruit. Pour and spoon into the loaf pan. Level the top.

Bake for about one hour, until golden in color and springy to the touch. Turn out of the pan and let cool on a wire rack.

P *** E * A *
PLANT OESTROGENS ARE PRESENT IN THE SOY AND WHOLE-WHEAT FLOURS, THE NUTS BRING EFAS AND THE APRICOTS PROVIDE ANTIOXIDANTS.

nutty gingerbread

This is a fragrant and irresistible bread, perfect for Christmas and cold winter evenings. The soy milk and flour in this version give phytoestrogens and the two kinds of nuts provide essential oils. Ginger is not only a warming spice, but is also beneficial for the circulation.

Butter or olive oil for greasing
¾ stick butter
4 tablespoons soy milk
2 eggs
¾ cup date syrup
1 cup whole-wheat self-rising flour
¼ cup soy flour
1 teaspoon sodium bicarbonate
1 tablespoon ground ginger
1 teaspoon ground cinnamon
½ teaspoon ground mixed spice
¼ cup almonds, chopped
¼ cup walnuts, chopped

Makes about 16 small squares

Preheat the oven to 350°F and grease a nine-inch square cake pan. Line it with parchment paper and grease that too. Heat the milk and melt the butter in it, then let cool to lukewarm. Whisk in the egg and date syrup until combined.

Sift the flours, sodium bicarbonate, and spices into a large bowl. Stir in the chopped nuts. Make a well in the center. Pour the milk mixture into the well and stir together until a smooth batter forms.

Pour into the pan and smooth the top. Bake for 30–40 minutes, until a skewer inserted comes out dry. Allow to cool on a wire rack. Turn out of the pan, remove the paper, and cut into squares to serve.

P **** E ** A *
PHYTOESTROGENS ARE SUPPLIED BY THE SOY MILK AND SOY FLOUR, AND EFAS FROM THE WALNUTS AND ALMONDS.

chocolate brownies

These brownies are for a special treat but are still much healthier than store-bought ones. The soy and whole-wheat flours give phytoestrogens and the nuts essential oils. As the nuts are cooked inside the brownies, the quality of the oils is somewhat protected from heat, which destroys valuable nutrients.

1 stick butter, plus more for greasing
2 ounces 100 percent cocoa powder, sifted
Large pinch of freshly ground salt
1 teaspoon baking powder
3 eggs (at room temperature), beaten
1⅓ cups date or maple syrup
2 teaspoons vanilla extract
¾ cup whole-wheat flour, sifted
2 heaped tablespoons soy flour, sifted
¾ cup pecan nuts, coarsely chopped
¾ cup dates, coarsely chopped

Makes about 30

Preheat the oven to 350°F and butter a 9 x 12-inch cake pan.

In a large mixing bowl, cream together the butter and cocoa powder until smooth. Beat in the salt and baking powder, followed by the eggs a little at a time, and continue to beat until well creamed. Add the date or maple syrup and vanilla and combine quickly with a few stirs of the spoon.

While this mixture is still streaky, fold in the flours and then, while that is still streaky, gently stir in the nuts and dates. Spoon into the prepared pan.

Bake for 25 minutes and leave to cool in the pan. Turn out and cut into bars to serve.

P *** E ** A *
PHYTOESTROGENS ARE SUPPLIED BY THE SOY AND WHOLE-WHEAT FLOURS AND THE NUTS BRING ESSENTIAL OILS.

fruity halvah

These Middle-Eastern bars make a delicious, healthy snack as well as a dessert. They contain sesame seeds, which are rich in calcium. Sesame seeds are also phytoestrogenic, as are the soy milk and cinnamon. Try to favor dried fruit that almost crystallizes when dried, like dates and pineapple.

1 cup honey
4 cups soy milk
1¾ sticks butter
1¾ cups fine semolina
3 ounces sesame seeds
Large pinch of ground cinnamon
3½ ounces mixed dried fruit, finely chopped

Makes about 36 bars

Make a syrup by mixing the honey and the milk and bringing to a boil, stirring all the time, then boil for about 15 minutes.

In a large heavy-bottomed saucepan, melt the butter over a low heat and add the semolina, seeds, and cinnamon. Cook, stirring constantly, until the seeds brown lightly. Add the milk syrup and stir to mix. Cover and simmer for five minutes, until it develops the consistency of a thick paste. Let cool slightly.

Stir in the dried fruit and pour out over a baking sheet lined with rice paper. Use a wetted palette knife to spread it over the paper in a flat rectangle. Cover with another piece of rice paper and weight this down with a tray and some cans. Leave it in a cool place for a few hours or overnight.

Cut into long bars to serve.

P *** E *** A *
PHYTOESTROGENS ARE IN GOOD SUPPLY FROM THE SESAME SEEDS, SOY MILK, AND CINNAMON. EFAS COME FROM THE SESAME SEEDS.

oatcakes

You can buy ready-made oatcakes from supermarkets and health food stores but they do not taste nearly as good as these, which are very easy to make. Oats are phytoestrogenic and, with their facility for lowering cholesterol, are also excellent for the heart. They are also a good source of fiber and will make a satisfying snack.

Olive oil or butter, for greasing
5 cups medium oatmeal, plus more for dusting
1 teaspoon freshly ground sea salt
1 teaspoon sodium bicarbonate
1 stick butter, melted
About ⅔ cup hot water

Makes 24

Preheat the oven to 300°F and then lightly grease two large baking sheets.

Mix the oatmeal, salt, and sodium bicarbonate in a mixing bowl. Stir in the melted butter and then pour in just enough of the water to bind the mixture to a firm dough.

On a surface dusted with more oatmeal, knead the dough briefly to remove cracks, then divide it into six pieces. Roll each of these out to a round about a quarter-inch thick and eight inches across. Cut each of these into quarters, brush off any loose oatmeal and arrange on the prepared baking sheets.

Bake for about 30 minutes, until firm and crisp. Allow to cool on wire racks.

P *** E * A *
PHYTOESTROGENS ARE SUPPLIED BY THE LARGE AMOUNTS OF OATMEAL.

sugarless sponge

This treat is not naughty but is very nice! Turn the sponge into a trifle using sugar-free jelly, fresh fruit, and natural custard powder (see page 40 for details). Or simply split the sponge and fill it with sugar-free jelly or lemon frosting (see to the right).

¾ stick slightly salted butter, plus more for the pan

1 cup all-purpose flour, plus more for dusting
3 large eggs
6 tablespoons honey

Makes a 9-in round sponge

Preheat the oven to 350°F. Butter the insides of a 9-inch cake pan, then line it with parchment paper and butter that. Dust the insides of the lined pan with flour, and shake out any excess.

Warm the butter gently until just pourable but not oiling; let it cool slightly. Sift the flour into a bowl. In another bowl set over a pan of hot water, whisk the eggs with the honey until the mixture is thick and the whisk leaves a trail when lifted. Take it off the heat.

Sift one-third of the flour into the egg mixture and fold it in as lightly as possible. Repeat with two more batches of flour. Fold a little of this batter into the softened butter and then fold that back into the batter.

Pour into the prepared pan and bake for 25–35 minutes, until the cake starts to shrink from the edges of the pan.

Run a knife around the edge of the pan to loosen the sponge, turn it out, and let cool on a wire rack before removing the lining papers.

Variations: you can give extra flavor – and phytoestrogens – to the basic sponge in lots of ways by adding to the batter: the grated peel of a lemon or orange, two teaspoons of ground cinnamon or one tablespoon of lightly toasted fennel seeds or caraway seeds.

P *** E * A *
FILLING THE CAKE WITH TOFU CREAM (SEE PAGE 155) WILL BOOST THE PHYTOE-STROGEN CONTENT.

carrot and olive oil cake

With its high antioxidant content, carrot cake is good for combating free radicals and preventing premature aging. The important antioxidant beta-carotene is present in the carrots, as well as the apples and orange juice. The carrots, soy flour, and tofu produce very high phytoestrogen levels here.

⅔ cup olive oil, plus more for greasing
⅔ cup whole-wheat flour
¾ cup all-purpose flour
2 tablespoons soy flour
1 scant tablespoon baking powder
2 teaspoons ground cinnamon
½ teaspoon freshly ground sea salt
⅔ cup honey
3 eggs, lightly beaten

Makes an 8-in cake

2 teaspoons vanilla extract
Grated peel of ½ orange
⅔ cup chopped walnuts, plus some unchopped walnut halves to decorate
6 ounces carrots, finely grated
2 sweet dessert apples, grated

For the lemon frosting
4 ounces soft tofu
1 teaspoon tahini
4 tablespoons maple syrup, or to taste
3 tablespoons lemon juice

Preheat the oven to 350°F, line an 8-inch cake pan with parchment paper, then oil the paper. Sift the flours, baking powder, cinnamon, and salt into a large mixing bowl (tossing in the granules left in the sifter at the end).

In another large mixing bowl, mix the oil with the honey, eggs, vanilla, and orange peel. Add to the flour mixture and blend in well. Fold in the nuts and grated carrots and apples.

Pour into the prepared pan and bake for about one hour, until a skewer inserted into the cake comes out clean.

Let cool in the cake pan for about 15 minutes, then turn out, remove the paper, and let cool completely on a wire rack.

While it is cooling, make the lemon frosting: put all the ingredients in a blender or food processor and process until smooth. When the cake is cool, spread this frosting over the top and decorate with some walnut halves. Leave at room temperature for an hour to let the frosting firm up a little.

P ***** E *** A ****

date baklava

This lovely dessert contains three different kinds of nuts, which are good sources of essential fatty acids. Dates are high in magnesium ("nature's tranquilizer") as well as potassium, which is so useful in preventing water retention and they will give the baklava an irresistibly moist and sticky taste.

Olive oil or butter, for greasing
¾ cup walnut halves
⅔ cup blanched almonds, lightly toasted in a dry skillet
⅔ cup pistachios, shelled and chopped
15 sheets of phyllo pastry
1 stick butter, melted
1½ cups dates, coarsely chopped
1 tablespoon honey
½ teaspoon ground cinnamon

For the syrup
1¾ cups date syrup
½ teaspoon ground cinnamon
Small pinch of ground cloves
Juice and grated peel of ½ small lemon
2 tablespoons orange flower water

Makes about 60 pieces

Preheat the oven to 325°F and generously grease the insides of a deep 8-inch square cake pan.

Put the walnuts, almonds, and pistachios in a food processor and pulse until reduced to the consistency of small bread crumbs.

Cut the sheets of phyllo roughly to the size of the cake pan, keeping them under a damp dish towel when not in use or they will dry out and become brittle. Arrange three sheets in the bottom of the pan, painting each with melted butter, and trimming as necessary.

Mix together the ground nuts, dates, honey, and cinnamon. Sprinkle one-quarter of this mixture over the phyllo base.

Continue with layers of buttered phyllo sheets and nut mixture until all are used up, finishing with a final three layers of buttered phyllo. Brush the top of this thoroughly with butter and sprinkle with a tablespoon of water.

Bake for 45 minutes, then increase the heat to 425°F and cook for a further 10–15 minutes, until puffed up and a light golden color.

During this last phase of cooking, mix together all the syrup ingredients in a pan and bring to a simmer. Simmer gently for about 10 minutes. As soon as the baklava comes out of the oven, pour this syrup mixture over it, and let cool in the pan

To serve, slice at angles to make 1-inch long rectangular shapes.

P* E** A*
THE WALNUTS, ALMONDS, AND PISTACHIOS IN THIS RECIPE PROVIDE GOOD AMOUNTS OF ESSENTIAL FATTY ACIDS.

8

basic recipes

basic vinaigrette

The flaxseed oil of this vinaigrette delivers a good punch of essential oils. Use wine vinegar (white or red), balsamic vinegar or lemon juice according to what best suits the salad ingredients. Other phyto-packed dressings: Crushed Nut Vinaigrette (page 76), Parsley Vinaigrette (page 117) and Lemon Vinaigrette (page 104).

3 tablespoons olive oil
2 tablespoons flaxseed oil
1 tablespoon wine vinegar or balsamic vinegar, or lemon juice
Freshly ground sea salt and black pepper

Makes about ⅛ cup

Either beat all the ingredients together in a bowl using a fork or shake in a screwtop jar to emulsify. When adding the seasoning to taste, add only just enough salt so that the dressing no longer tastes oily.

P * E ***** A **

miso broth

A great store of phytoestrogens, from the miso (soybean paste), parsley and garlic. Add miso to stews and soups by mixing a tablespoon of miso into a bowl with hot water, then adding back to the dish. Once miso has been added to the dish, do not boil, or its beneficial enzymes will be lost.

1 small onion or 2–3 shallots, chopped
1 garlic clove, chopped
Handful of parsley stalks (without the leaves)
1 tablespoon miso

Makes about 3½ cups

Boil up four cups of water with the onion, garlic, and parsley, then lower the heat, cover, and simmer for about 30 minutes to an hour. After this, pour a little broth into a small bowl, and stir in the miso. Add to the saucepan of broth and stir well.

Variations: try adding a few slices of ginger with the onion and garlic for Asian dishes. Miso broth is also tasty with added seaweed kombu, which brings extra nutrients.

P ***** E * A **

sesame tofu dressing

This creamy dressing works well on most salads and lightly cooked vegetables and is rich in phytos and EFAs. If you cannot get white miso from healthfood stores, add some soy sauce.

4 ounces soft tofu
2 tablespoons sesame oil
1 tablespoon flaxseed oil
2½ tablespoons cider vinegar
2 teaspoons white miso or soy sauce
1 garlic clove, crushed
1 tablespoon mirin (Japanese rice wine)
1 tablespoon sesame seeds, lightly toasted

Makes about 1 cup

Put all the ingredients except the sesame seeds in a blender or food processor and process until smooth. Stir in the sesame seeds to finish.

P ***** E *** A *

court-bouillon

Use this aromatic liquid for poaching fish, as it both adds flavor and minimizes any flavor lost from the fish to the liquid.

1 onion, chopped
2 celery stalks, chopped
2 carrots, chopped
⅔ cup dry white wine
1 bay leaf
Juice of ½ lemon
1 teaspoon black peppercorns
Freshly ground sea salt

Makes about 5¼ pints

Put all the ingredients in a large saucepan with four and a half pints of water. Bring to a boil and boil for about 10 minutes, skimming, then leave to cool slightly.

Season to taste with salt, and then strain over the fish to be cooked.

P ** E * A **

vegetable stock

This stock keeps well, covered, in the refrigerator for up to a week or frozen for up to a month.
If you are going to reduce it down for a sauce, etc., don't add any salt. Be careful not to use too much of any one stronger-flavored vegetable like fennel, cabbage, or leek, or it may overpower the other flavors.

4 pounds mixed vegetables, preferably including carrots, onions, broccoli, green beans, celery stalks, and tomatoes, coarsely chopped
Large handful of parsley stalks, chopped
1 garlic clove, cut in half (optional)
1 small red chile (optional)
1 bay leaf
1 teaspoon black peppercorns
⅔ cup dry white wine
Freshly ground sea salt

Makes about 5¼ pints

Put all the ingredients except the salt in a large pot, add seven pints of cold water and bring to a boil.

Reduce the heat to a gentle simmer and cook gently, uncovered, for about an hour.

Strain through a fine strainer, discarding the solids, and season to taste with salt.

P ** E * A **
AN EXCELLENT VARIETY OF ANTIOXIDANTS FROM THE VEGETABLES AND ALSO PHYTOESTROGENS FROM THE BROCCOLI, CARROTS, AND THE CELERY.

fish/seafood stock

If you buy your fish from a good old-fashioned fishmonger they are usually only too happy to supply you with the trimmings from your fish – and any others that happen to be lying around. Try to avoid trimmings from oily fish like mackerel – even salmon – as these give too strong a flavor.

2¼ pounds fish or seafood trimmings, such as bones, heads (gills removed), tails, shells, etc.
1 onion, chopped
2 fennel stalks, chopped
2 carrots, chopped
Large handful of parsley stalks, chopped
⅔ cup dry white wine
Juice of ½ lemon
1 teaspoon black peppercorns
Freshly ground sea salt

Makes about 1½ pints

Thoroughly rinse the fish trimmings and put them in a large pot with the remaining ingredients, except salt, and one and three-quarter pints of cold water. Bring to a boil slowly and skim carefully.

Lower the heat and simmer gently for 30 minutes (no more or the fish bones will start to give off bitterness), skimming from time to time.

Strain through a fine strainer, discarding the solids, and season to taste with salt.

**P ** E * A **
THE FENNEL, CARROTS, AND PARSLEY IN THE STOCK ALL OFFER PHYTOE-STROGENS, AND THE CARROTS ARE RICH IN THE IMPORTANT ANTIOXIDANT, BETA-CAROTENE.

basic tomato sauce

This keeps well in a covered container in the refrigerator for up to a week. Packed full of antioxidants from the lycopene in the tomatoes, the sauce also contains phytoestrogens from the miso, garlic, and parsley. Use this as a base for pasta dishes, stews, and chili con carne.

2 tablespoons olive oil
1 large onion, chopped
1 garlic clove, finely chopped
1/3–1/2 cup red wine (optional)
14 ounces canned chopped plum tomatoes
3 tablespoons tomato paste
1 tablespoon parsley, chopped
1–2 teaspoons miso dissolved in 1¼ cups boiling water
Freshly ground sea salt and black pepper

Makes about 2 pounds

Heat the oil in a heavy-bottomed saucepan and sauté the onion in it gently until just translucent, then add the garlic, and sauté for about a minute more. Add the wine (if using) and boil rapidly to reduce it to a sticky liquid.

Stir in the tomatoes with their liquid, the tomato paste, parsley, and miso broth. Mix well, season, and simmer for about 30 minutes, until it has a thick sauce-like consistency.

P *** E * A ****
THE MISO, GARLIC, AND PARSLEY DELIVER PHYTOESTROGENS AND TOMATOES CONTAIN IMPORTANT ANTIOXIDANTS.

tomato ketchup

Ketchup is a staple of nearly every household's cupboard, but the store-bought version is unfortunately full of sugar. This version is much better for you, and so much better tasting. It will keep for one to two weeks in the refrigerator, covered. Other health-giving ingredients include the ginger, which is good for circulation.

Two 14-ounce cans of chopped plum tomatoes
1 onion, finely chopped
1 garlic clove, very finely chopped
3 tablespoons cider vinegar
3 tablespoons red wine (optional)
3 tablespoons tomato paste
3 tablespoons honey
1 teaspoon finely grated fresh ginger or 2 teaspoons
    ground dried ginger
Good pinch of ground allspice
Good pinch of ground cloves
Good pinch of ground mace
Good pinch of celery salt
Freshly ground sea salt and black pepper

Makes about 1 pound

Puree the tomatoes with the onion and garlic in a food processor until smooth (you may need to do this in batches). Tip into a heavy-bottomed saucepan and stir in the remaining ingredients with seasoning to taste. Bring to a simmer and cook gently for 30 minutes, or until nice and thick, stirring from time to time.

P * E * A ****
HIGH LEVELS OF ANTIOXIDANTS FROM THE TOMATOES AND RED WINE IN PARTICULAR.

blender mayonnaise

This unusual mayonnaise is made with flaxseed oil, which is high in EFAs. As mayonnaise is made from raw eggs, you do have to be careful about possible salmonella levels. Use fresh eggs bought from a reliable supplier, and keep it (and dishes made using it) in the fridge for no more than a day or two.

½ cup olive oil
½ cup flaxseed oil
1 large egg
Pinch of dry mustard powder
Freshly ground sea salt and black pepper
1 tablespoon cider vinegar or lemon juice
1 tablespoon boiling water

Makes about 1¼ cups

Try to ensure that all the ingredients are at the same room temperature before you begin. In a jug, mix the oils together.

Put the egg and mustard powder in the (ideally small inner) bowl of the food processor with seasoning to taste. Process until foaming, then add the cider vinegar or lemon juice and pulse to mix. With the machine running, dribble in the mixed oils, almost drop by drop to begin with and then in a slow steady stream, pouring faster as the mayonnaise starts to thicken. Mix in the boiling water at the end to help make the mayonnaise more stable. To be really safe, it's really not advisable to serve raw egg to young children, pregnant women or invalids.

Variation: basic mayonnaise can be flavored in a myriad of ways to suit different food: try adding two or three garlic cloves with the egg for a garlic mayonnaise that is wonderful with shrimp or crudités; stir in some chopped parsley, chives, and chervil at the end for a herb mayonnaise that goes with most fish and egg dishes; whizz in a bunch of watercress to make the most unforgettable dressing for boiled potatoes. (Also see Remoulade Dressing, page 118.)

P * E **** A *
FLAXSEED OIL DELIVERS VALUABLE ESSENTIAL FATTY ACIDS.

soy mayonnaise

While not strictly a mayonnaise (it is also much easier to make), this makes an excellent creamy dressing and is also rich in phytoestrogens, with its tofu and linseed oil content. Garlic is believed to have cancer-inhibiting properties and will help to lower blood cholesterol levels.

5 ounces soft tofu
4 tablespoons olive oil
4 tablespoons linseed oil
1 tablespoon soy sauce
2 garlic cloves, crushed
1 teaspoon Tabasco sauce
1 tablespoon lemon juice
Freshly ground sea salt and black pepper

Makes about ⅓ cup

Put all the ingredients in a blender or food processor and process until smooth, seasoning to taste.

P **** E *** A *
THIS DISH IS HIGH IN PHYTOESTROGENS FROM THE TOFU AND LINSEED OIL.
EFAS ARE SUPPLIED BY THE OLIVE OIL AND LINSEED OIL.

pesto sauce

Pesto is a useful thing–it makes a tasty dressing for vegetable dishes and an easy pasta sauce. You get the best results by using a pestle and mortar, but you can mix everything but the cheese in a blender and then stir in the cheese at the end.

2 ounces basil (about 1 cup)
¼ cup pine nuts
2 garlic cloves

Freshly ground sea salt and
 black pepper
1½ cups Parmesan cheese,
 freshly grated
6 tablespoons flaxseed oil
6 tablespoons olive oil

**Makes about 14 ounces
(12 good dollops)**

Using a pestle and mortar, pound the basil, pine nuts, garlic, and a pinch of salt to a paste.

Mix in the cheese well, then beat in the oils, a little at a time. Adjust the seasoning with salt and, if you like although it is not strictly necessary, a little pepper.

Variations: these days pestos crop up made from all sorts of things; most commonly the basil is replaced with either parsley, cilantro, or anchovy.

P *   E ****   A *
AN EXCELLENT SELECTION OF EFAS FROM THE FLAXSEED OIL AND PINE NUTS.

tofu dip for raw vegetables

1 tablespoon sesame oil
1 teaspoon flaxseed oil
Freshly ground sea salt
½ teaspoon grated ginger
8 ounces soft tofu

Serves 4

Put all the ingredients in a blender or food processor and blend until smooth, adding just enough water, a little at a time, to get a good dipping consistency.

Variation: you can add a tablespoon or two of tahini for even more flavor and goodness.

P ****   E ****   A ****

herb butters

These butters are wonderfully handy to have in the fridge; they make an easy dressing for broiled fish and are great on broiled or boiled vegetables. You could mix herbs, such as parsley, chervil, chives, and tarragon or use finely chopped garlic, chile, or ginger instead. Try herb butters as an instant omelet filling or pasta sauce.

Handful of herb leaves (see above), finely chopped
Freshly ground sea salt and black pepper
1 stick softened unsalted butter

Makes about 5 ounces – 10 pats

In a small bowl and using a fork, mash the herb(s) with seasoning to taste into the butter. Turn out on a sheet of waxed paper and roll into a cylinder. Chill until firm.

To use, cut off half-ounce slices as required.

Variations: Mix in some flaxseed oil as you are mashing the herbs into the butter to boost the nutrition content.

P ****   E ***   A **

peanut butter

It is best to keep this nutty spread in the refrigerator and use within a couple of days: you won't find this hard, as it is so tempting. It is full of essential oils, from the flaxseed oil.

8 ounces skinned raw peanuts
4 tablespoons flaxseed oil
Freshly ground sea salt

Makes about 9 ounces

Gently dry-roast the peanuts in a skillet; do not burn. Allow to cool. In a blender or food processor, process the nuts and oil together to a paste (coarse or smooth as you prefer). Season to taste with salt.

P **   E ****   A *

peanut sauce

This sauce is rich in nutritional goodies and full of taste. The soy milk and garlic contain high amounts of phytoestrogens, and the onions have a positive influence on bone health and the garlic is an anti-cancer ingredient. Use the sauce within a couple of days, and store it in the refrigerator.

1 large red onion, coarsely chopped
3 garlic cloves
1–2 fresh red chiles, seeded (optional)
6 ounces skinned raw peanuts
2 tablespoons olive oil
1 tablespoon soy sauce
2 tablespoons tamarind paste, dissolved in 2 tablespoons water
⅔ cup soy milk
2 teaspoons honey
Freshly ground sea salt

Makes about 1¾ cups

Blend the onion, garlic, and chile (if using) in a blender or food processor until they form a paste.

Gently dry-roast the peanuts in a skillet, stirring to avoid burning. Let cool. When they are cool, crush them in a food processor until finely ground.

Heat the oil in a wok. Add the onion paste and fry, stirring constantly, for one minute. Add the ground peanuts and continue stirring until combined. Add the soy sauce, tamarind, soy milk, and honey.

Gently cook until all the flavors are combined and a thickish sauce has formed (add a little water if necessary), about 15 minutes. Add salt to taste.

P **** E ** A **
GOOD QUANTITIES OF PHYTOESTROGENS IN THE SOY MILK AND GARLIC; ESSENTIAL OILS FROM THE PEANUTS.

mocha tofu cream

This is a delicious coffee-flavored "cream" but without the usual heavy calories and saturated fat. It is rich in plant estrogens from the tofu and essential oils from the almond butter. The raisins contain a good amount of potassium, is necessary for good heart function and also helps with water retention.

½ cup raisins
8 ounces silken tofu
3 tablespoons almond butter
1 tablespoon instant coffee
Pinch of freshly ground sea salt

Serves 2

Put the raisins in a saucepan with water to cover. Bring to a simmer and cook gently for 20 minutes. Drain the raisins and blend until smooth.

Squeeze as much water from the tofu as you can. In a blender or food processor, process the tofu, the raisin puree, the almond butter, and the coffee granules until really smooth.

P **** E *** A **
THE TOFU PROVIDES THE PHYTOESTROGENS AND ALMONDS ARE A SOURCE OF EFAS.

tofu cream

This makes an excellent substitute for dairy cream and can be used as a topping for a fruit salad or on any desserts where you would normally use cream.

8 ounces soft tofu
½ teaspoon vanilla extract
⅓–½ cup maple syrup
1 tablespoon sunflower oil
1 teaspoon flaxseed oil

Serves 4

Combine all ingredients in a blender until smooth.

P **** E * A *
HIGH PHYTOESTROGEN CONTENT FROM THE TOFU AND FLAXSEED OIL.

references

Food and menopause
1 Writing Group for the Women's Health Initiative Investigator (2002), Risks and benefits of estrogen plus progestin in healthy postmenopausal women: principal results from the Women's Health Initiative randomized controlled trial, *Journal of the American Medical Association*, 288, 321–33 Division of Women's Health Initiative, National Heart, Lung, and Blood Institute, 6705 Rockledge Dr, One Rockledge Ctr, Suite 300, Bethesda, MD 20817, USA

Understanding the role of estrogen
1 as above

What you need to eat during menopause
1 de Kleijn MJ et al, Intake of dietary phytoestrogens is low in postmenopausal women in the United States: the Framingham study, *Journal of Nutrition* (2001), 131, 6, 1826–32
2 Anderson JJB et al, Health potential of soy isoflavones for menopausal women, *Public Health Nutrition* (1999), 2, 4, 489–504
3 A Murkies et al, 'Dietary flour supplementation decreases postmenopausal hot flashes: effect of soy and wheat', *Maturitas–Journal of the Climacteric and Postmenopause* (1995), 21, 189-195
4 P Albertazzi et al, 'The effect of dietary soy-supplementation on hot flashes', *Obstetrics and Gynaecology* (1998), 91, 1
5 G Wilcox et al, 'Estrogenic effects of plant foods in postmenopausal women', *British Medical Journal* (1990), 905–906
6 Source: US National Cancer Institute
7 J Ziegler, 'Soybeans show promise in cancer prevention', *Journal of the National Cancer Institute* (1994), 86, 1666–1667
8 H Aldercreutz et al, 'Dietary phytoestrogens and cancer: *in vitro* and *in vivo* studies', *Journal of Steroid Biochemistry and Molecular Biology* (1992), 3–8, 41, 331–337
9 SP Verma, 'Curcumin and genistein, plant natural products, show synergistic inhibitory effects on the growth of breast cancer MCF-7 cells', *Biophysical Research Communications* (1997), 23, 3, 692, 696
10 C Gennari, 'Introduction to the Symposium', *Bone Mineral* (1992), 19, S1–S2 and JB Anderson et al, 'The effects of phytoestrogens on bone', *Nutrition Research* (1997), 17, 10, 1617–1632

11 FS Dalias et al, 'Dietary soy supplementation increases vaginal cytology maturation index and bone mineral content in postmenopausal women', Second International Symposium on the Role of Soy in Preventing and Treating Chronic Disease (1996, Brussels, Belgium)
12 HM Linkswiler et al, 'Protein-induced hypercalciuria', *Federation Proceedings* (1981), 40, 2429–2433 and BJ Abelow et al, 'Cross-cultural association between dietary animal protein and hip fracture: a hypothesis', *Calcified Tissue International* (1992), 50, 14–18
13 Source: M Messina et al, *The Simple Soybean and Your Health* (1994, Avery Publishing, New York)
14 NA Breslau et al, 'Relationship of animal protein-rich diet to kidney stone formation and calcium metabolism', *Journal of Clinical Andocrincology and Metabolism* (1988), 66, 140–146
15 MJ Stampfer et al, *New England Journal of Medicine* (1985), 313, 1044–1049
16 Writing Group for the Women's Health Initiative Investigator (2002), Risks and benefits of estrogen plus progestin in healthy postmenopausal women: principal results from the Women's Health Initiative randomized controlled trial, *Journal of the American Medical Association*, 288, 321–33
17 J Anderson et al, 'Meta-analysis of the effects of soy protein intake on serum lipids' (1995), *New England Journal of Medicine*, 333, 5, 276–282
18 DE Pratt et al, 'Source of antioxidant activity of soybeans and soy products', *Journal of Food Science* (1979), 44, 1720–1722
19 G Dhom, 'Epidemiology of hormone-dependent tumors' in *Endocrine-Dependent Tumours*. KD Voigt and C Knabbe eds (1991, Raven Press, New York)
20 MS Morton et al, 'Lignans and isoflavonoids in plasma and prostatic fluid in men: samples from Portugal, Hong Kong and the United Kingdom', *The Prostate* (1997), 32, 122–128
21 SB Bittiner et al, 'A double-blind, randomized, placebo-controlled trial of fish oil in psoriasis', *The Lancet* (1985), 1, 378–380
22 J Kremer et al, 'Effects of manipulation of dietary fatty acids on clinical manifestation of

rheumatoid arthritis', *The Lancet* (1985), 1, 184–187 and F McCrae et al, 'Diet and Arthritis', *Practitioner* (1986), 230, 359–361
23 H Aldercreutz, 'Lignans and phytoestrogens: possible preventative role in cancer' in P Rozen ed. *Frontiers of Gastrointestinal Research*, Vol 14, (1988), Karger, Basel, Switzerland) 165–176
24 LB Taubman, 'Theories of Aging', *Resident and Staff Physician* (1986), 32, 31–37
25 AA Bertilli et al, 'Antiplatelet activity of cisresveratrol', *Drugs under Experimental and Clinical Research* (1996), 22, 2, 61–63
26 J Levt et al, 'Carotene and antioxidant vitamins in the prevention of oral cancer', *New York Academy of Sciences* (1992), 260–269
27 E Middleton and G Drzewieki, 'Naturally occurring flavonoids and human basophil histamine release', *International Archives of Allergy and Applied Immunology* (1985), 77, 155–157
28 M Gabor, 'Pharmacologic effects of flavonoids on blood vessels', *Angiologica* (1972), 9, 355–374
29 JD Cohen and HW Rubin, 'Functional menorrhagia: treatment with bioflavonoids and vitamin C', *Current Therapeutic Research* (1960), 2, 539–542
30 J Monboisse et al, 'Oxygen: free radicals as mediators of collagen breakage', *Agents Actions* (1984), 15, 49–50
31 GE Abraham, *Journal of Nutritional Medicine* (1991), 2, 165–178
32 AK Bordia et al, 'Effect of garlic oil on patient with CHD', *Artherosclerosis* (1977), 28, 155–159
33 I Yamamoto et al, 'Anti-tumor effects of seaweed', *Japanese Journal of Experimental Medicine* (1974), 44, 543–546
34 N Iritani and S Nagi, 'Effects of spinach and wakame on cholesterol turnover in the rat', *Atherosclerosis* (1972), 15, 87–92

What you don't need during menopause
1 TL Holbrook and E Barrett-Conner, *British Medical Journal* (1993), 1056–1058
2 A Komori et al, 'Anticarcinogenic activity of green tea polyphenols', *Japanese Journal of Clinical Oncology* (1993), 23, 3, 186–190

shopper's guide

The following are organic food stores–some are able to send products by mail order:

4th Street Food Co-op, 58 East 48th St. New York, New York 10003
212-674-3623

Amigo's Natural Grocery, 326 Paseo Del Pueblo Sur, Taos, New Mexico 87571
505-758-8493

Ashland Community Food Store, 237 N. 1st St., Ashland, Oregon 97520
503-482-2237

Blooming Prairie Natural Foods, 510 Kasota Ave. SE, Minneapolis, Minnesota 55414
612-378-9774

Chico Natural Foods, 818 Main Street Chico, California 95928,
530-891-1713

Corners of the Mouth Natural Foods, 45015 Ukiah St., Mendocino, California 95460,
707-937-5345

Deep Roots Market, 3728 Spring Garden St. Greensboro, North Carolina 27407
336-292-9216

Green Star Cooperative Market, 710 West Buffalo St., Ithaca, New York 14850
607-273-9392

The Natural Health Practice
orders@naturalhealthpractice.com
Suppliers of Menoplus (see page 39)

Outpost Natural Foods Co-op, 100 E. Capital Dr., Milwaukee, Wisconsin 53212
414-961-2597

People's Natural Food Store, 3029 SE. 21st St., Portland, Oregon 97202
503-232-9051

Rainbow Grocery, 417 15th Ave. E, Seattle, Washington
206-329-8440

Rainbow Groceries, 1745 Folsom, San Francisco, California 94103
415-863-0621

Smart Food Co-op, 69 First St., Cambridge, Massachusetts 02141
617-576-9460

Stone Soup Chicago, 4637 N. Ashland Ave, Chicago, Illinois 60640
773-506-2465

Venice Ocean Park Food Co-op, 839 Lincoln Blvd., Venice, California 90291
310-399-5623

Whole Foods Co-op, 119 W. 21st St., Norfolk, Virginia 23517
757-626-1051

staying in touch

If you have any health problems and are interested in finding a more natural approach to treating them, or would like to find out what supplements and tests are available to you, please feel free to contact my clinic for more information.

Consultations
If you would like help with any personal health problems, private consultations are available at my clinics in London or Tunbridge Wells clinics. Postal consultations are also available. For appointments and enquiries contact:

Dr Marilyn Glenville, 14 St John's Road, Tunbridge Wells, Kent TN4 9NP, England
Int. Tel: +44 1892 515905
Int. Fax: +44 1892 515914
Website: www.marilynglenville.com
Email: health@marilynglenville.com

index

resources

American Menopause Foundation
866 United Nations Plaza, Suite 508
New York, NY 10017
212-714-2398
www.americanmenopause.org

The North American Menopause Society
5900 Landerbrook Drive, Suite 390
Mayfield Heights, OH 44124
440-442-7550
www.menopause.org

National Women's Health
Resource Center
157 Broad Street, Suite 106
Red Bank, NJ 07701
1-877-986-9472
www.healthywomen.org

National Institutes of Health
9000 Rockville Pike
Bethesda, MD 20892
301-496-4000
www.nih.gov

American Heart Association
National Center
7272 Greenville Avenue
Dallas, TX 75231
1-800-AHA-USA-1 (1-800-242-8721)
www.americanheart.org

U.S. Department of Health & Human
Services
200 Independence Avenue, S.W.
Washington, D.C. 20201
1-877-696-6775
www.healthfinder.gov

The Gerald J. and Dorothy R. Friedman
School of Nutrition Science and Policy at
Tufts University
150 Harrison Avenue
Boston, MA 02111
617-636-2940
www.nutrition.tufts.edu

USDA Food and Nutrition Information
Center
National Agricultural Library
10301 Baltimore Avenue, Room 105
Beltsville, MD 20705
301-504-5414
www.nutrition.gov

Centers for Disease Control and
Prevention
1600 Clifton Road
Atlanta, GA 30333
1-800-CDC-INFO (1-800-232-4636)
www.cdc.gov

acknowledgements

This book would not have been written
without the help and support of friends and
colleagues.

I would particularly like to thank Lewis Esson
for the invaluable contribution to the recipes
and for his ability to incorporate unusual
ingredients to make such delicious dishes. I
would also like to express my appreciation to
Kyle Cathie and her superb team for all their
support and encouragement.

My thanks also go to all the support staff at
my office who have been working in the
background, making it possible for me to
complete this book.

My love goes to my family Kriss, Matt,
Len, and Chantell for all their support
and continued interest in whatever I am
working on.

Recipe photographs shown outside the
recipe section are as follows:

p1 Fruit tart (recipe on p130)
p2 Sushi rolls (recipe on p106)
p38 Vegetable, beansprout and tofu stir-fry
(recipe on p89)

All photographs by Ian Wallace except for
the following:
Will Heap: pp 4/44, 4/72, 5/108, 5/148, 13, 23
Peter Cassidy: pp 4/84, 21, 24
Gus Filgate: pp 4/56, 5/122